Interviewing for
the Decisionmaker

Interviewing for the Decisionmaker

Lawrence R. O'Leary

Nelson-Hall nh Chicago

Library of Congress Cataloging in Publication Data

O'Leary, Lawrence R
    Interviewing for the decisionmaker.
    Includes index.
    1. Employment interviewing.   I. Title.
HF5549.5.I6037   658.31'12   75-44322
ISBN 0-88229-215-3

Manufactured in the United States of America

*To my wife, Gerty, and
my daughters, Elizabeth,
Julia, and Bridgette*

Contents

Foreword

Business firms, and organizations in other sectors as well, have only recently come to recognize their human resources as a business asset that requires attention of the first order. A decade or so ago, it was commonplace to find board room or front office thinking which basically subordinated the people end of the business to the traditional technology, equipment, product, marketing, and capital structure emphasis. The behavioral scientists, civil rights legislation, and the emergence of changing lifestyles have caused forward thinking managers to recognize that to generate positive, sustained momentum in any organization, human resources must be placed on an equal footing with other assets. In this book, Dr. Lawrence O'Leary presents reasoned and practical approaches to personnel selection—the genesis in people-power management for organization effectiveness.

Selecting employment candidates and considering current employees for promotion are and always will be somewhat of a gamble. Unfortunately, too often they are not dissimilar to rolling the dice. That can be true for the manager-owner of a small business who may have one or two employment openings a year as well as the professional interviewer and hiring manager who staff a multiplicity of positions every month. The key here is to shift the odds whereby the best possible staffing decisions may be made in the greater majority of instances, if not all the time. This qualification references the fact that on occasion, albeit infrequent, the most seasoned employment professional will misjudge a candidate's qualifications against the position specifications. Now more than ever before, hiring the best qualified candidate is a matter of factoring in the dimension of fair employment.

The problem up to now has been a paucity of identifiable handles or guidelines to a viable selection process. Yes, from time to time we obtain input from different sources as to theory or what works well in a particular organization; yet, it doesn't seem to quite fit our needs. Also, fair employment legislation has created questions in the minds of many as to just how far they can legally go in finding the best applicant.

How important is selection? There are many dimensions to consider such as product rejects or declining sales volume due to improper staffing, but stop and think a minute about one single element that affects all of us regardless of the organization or type of position in question—the cost of hiring, training, and replacing an unqualified employee. At the absolute minimum, we're looking at $1,000 in terms of the most basic job in which an employee hasn't measured up. The cost goes up to five or six figures when an inappropriate executive selection has been made. Several of these incidents can have a marked unfavorable effect on margins in most businesses. While recognizing the people business for what it is, a myriad of complex elements, we can aim for a selection process which reduces errors. To focus in, our objective becomes one of minimizing wrong decisions and maximizing right decisions.

The title of this book, *Interviewing for the Decisionmaker,* emphasizes the ROI (return on investment) which the reader may expect. Dr. O'Leary, in the decisionmaker's style, has taken the mystery out of the selection process and its key elements by providing a systems approach which makes sense. The guidelines he identifies are equally applicable to all people in any organization who find themselves making hiring or promotional decisions. The practicalness of his concepts will be particularly refreshing and meaningful for the busy line manager who is looking for a clear snapshot or road map of "how to." The personnel or industrial relations professional will find this book to be more than just a refresher. As an example, Dr. O'Leary examines the important subject of testing which too many of us have inappropriately sidestepped in the selection process due to fair employment legislation. His comments on tomorrow's personnel selection systems are thought provoking, particularly his treatment of Assessment Centers—an in-vogue technique of today which is bound to become amplified in the not too distant future.

Dr. O'Leary has fulfilled his desire that this book "bridge the gap between behavioral science on one hand, and day-to-day practical hiring decisions on the other." The theme throughout provides the reader with simple, practical tools to use with basic common sense. The treatment represents the "real life" world whether it be the shop floor, the office, or the executive suite.

CURTIS J. BROWN
Vice President, Industrial Relations
Bergen Brunswig Corporation

Introduction—
Fact and Fiction

You've undoubtedly seen the television show on which three individuals claim to be the real John Jones. A celebrity panel is given a brief biographical sketch of Jones and his exploits. By asking questions, each panelist tries to ferret out the real Jones or trip up the pretenders. Later, each signifies his choice of which interviewee was telling the truth. After a proper tension-building period, the real Jones stands up.

This scene is replayed thousands of times daily. Personnel professionals, line managers, social workers, counselors, police officers, credit managers, and army recruiters all conduct individual interviews with John Joneses. They place a lot of emphasis on a little interviewing. Their discussions form the basis for judgments about hiring, promotion, eligibility for loans and welfare payments, or assignment to the motor pool.

Unfortunately, once their decisions are made, the interviewers do not have the immediate "you were right—you were wrong" validation that the television program provides.

Indeed, there are no specific steps an interviewer can take to insure 100 percent accuracy in judging another individual. In fact, there is scant practical information available for interviewers. Thus it is that many individuals in the interviewing field have made themselves comfortable with one of the great fictions of modern business—that talking is interviewing.

On top of this, many officials now so fear violating the law against bias in hiring or promotion that they make no attempt whatsoever to find out what they can do to start validating their selection decisions.

The major legislation in this area is Title VII of the 1964 Civil Rights Act as amended by the 1972 Civil Rights Act. Essentially, this legislation makes it illegal to discriminate against minorities in hiring procedures. Protected classes under this legislation include Negroes, females, Orientals, Spanish surnamed people, and Indians.

More specifically, in those cases where a disproportionate number of minority persons are being eliminated, the law requires the employer to demonstrate that his selection procedure is valid (that his tests or interviews pick good personnel and eliminate poor work performance). The original act established a watchdog commission (the Equal Employment Opportunity Commission or EEOC) to investigate complaints of discrimination. Since 1964, when its original budget was $2.5 million, EEOC activity has grown considerably, a fact reflected in the size of its 1974 annual budget—$50 million.

So, while a down-to-earth, practical understanding of the process is sadly limited, interviewing, hiring, promoting people, and validating results are extremely important activities. Consider:

1. *Interviews are an integral part of the hiring decision.* Studies indicate that 99 percent of the de-

cisions to hire in today's business are preceded by a personal interview.

2. *Selection decisions are expensive.* A decision (based largely on an interview) to add one person to the payroll can cost thousands of dollars, even before the new staff member shows up for the first day's work.

3. *Finally, interviews and decisions are sensitive.* Recent fair employment legislation and rulings (Title VII of the 1964 Civil Rights Act, the *Griggs* v. *Duke Power* case, the Civil Rights Act of 1972) have served to increase the scrutiny being given to all selection procedures, including the interview. (In *Griggs* v. *Duke Power,* considered a landmark case, the Supreme Court unanimously ruled against an employer as discriminating in his hiring procedures.) Certain questions if asked of a job applicant now are clearly illegal (e.g., Have you ever been arrested?). Tests have to be validated. Many interviewers, particularly personnel professionals who make their living in this risky business, are not sure how far they can legally go to find the best applicant. This uncertainty has spread to company presidents, sales managers, plant managers, department heads, and even to Mom—that is, to the co-owner of the Mom and Pop store when she wants to hire a stockboy.

In a nutshell, I have described both the problems and the importance of interviewing and selecting people and validating the results.

The remainder of this book offers advice to two groups of people—those who interview and those who validate. The first part on interviewing is aimed at those millions of individuals who make selection or promotion decisions and who use interviews in the process. It presents guidelines for sound interviewing and describes what has been discovered about interviewing through empirical studies. Behavioral science findings have been applied to the development of both a systematic and flexible interview procedure.

For the busy line manager doing limited interviewing, the first four chapters should answer his immediate questions. Chapter 5 is designed to help the supervisor who must talk with troublesome subordinates. The second part of the book (chapters 6 through 8) deals with validating the selection interview.

The principles and techniques of successful interviewing presented here apply to all organizations on all levels. This book is addressed to anyone who finds himself making hiring and promotion decisions based at least in part on interviews. The top executive selecting an administrative assistant, controller, or general manager will find this study just as helpful as those persons hiring laundry workers, recruiting officers for the military, or choosing committees for union apprenticeship programs.

This is a book for the decisionmakers who must base their judgments on the interview.

I have used the generic form "he" throughout for succinctness. No sexism is intended.

chapter 1

The Interview
in Perspective

Interviewers can indulge in one luxury. They can read the plethora of books about why people behave the way they do. Books like *I'm OK, You're OK,* by Thomas Harris, and *Games People Play,* by Eric Berne, describe a promising new method of analyzing interpersonal behavior: transactional analysis. On a recent visit to Sangamon State University, a relatively new senior university in Illinois, I was surprised to learn there was a full-time instructor teaching nothing but the transactional approach to interviewing.

Also much written about is body language, another way to find out more about an individual. This approach may have some merit, but I suggest that more data be collected before the interpretation of body language can be considered a practical tool for the interviewer. A client told me recently about an "expert" who suggested that the examination of facial expressions was the best source of interview information. Focus on nuances of facial expressions, he suggested, and the real John Jones will be revealed to you.

More specific advice on interviewing has been directed to personnel and line managers. I have often come in contact with these instant success interview techniques when clients ask me what I think about this or that new approach.

A recent *Wall Street Journal* article also listed some of the techniques that executives have developed to hire and promote. Among them:

One executive insists on inspecting the glove compartment of an applicant's car "to see if it's a mess."

A top New York executive often dumps a glass of water into the lap of stodgy applicants to see how they react in stress situations.

A client of a Chicago executive recruiter refuses to hire anyone who holds the railing going up the stairs, figuring that's a sign of poor health.

The head of a midwestern concern who stands 5 feet 7 inches won't hire anyone taller than himself.

If an applicant has played football, one executive always rates quarterbacks over tackles.

Is there one right approach or one accurate measure of an individual's worthiness? I don't think so. When you review the literature covering the selection interview and critically compare it with what research findings are available, you find many of these fads just do not hold up under scientific scrutiny. In fact, the majority of my academic colleagues would echo the sentiments of Milton Blum and Jerry Naylor in their book, *Industrial Psychology—Its Theoretical and Social Foundations:* "There is so much to be done in the way of research on the interview that it is very difficult to make any recommendations on how to conduct the selection interview."

If there is no one-step solution, and if authors of industrial psychology texts tell students there is little or no meaningful research data, what am I doing writing this book? And what are you doing reading it?

The answer is that whether there are reams of or wretchedly little research on interviews, whether you have tried the "one right answer" approach or the "I have a feeling" technique, you still face decisions on hiring and promoting every day or every week. They don't go away.

If I can provide you with a good perspective of the interview and offer you some solid guidelines based on available research, I think I can help you to make better hiring and promotion decisions.

The Objective of a Selection Process

In theory, the objective of any selection process is to hire or promote the best applicant—always.

There is no infallible selection procedure. We've seen how some business people rely too much on one criterion to judge others. There is also a strong tendency for managers to downgrade any selection device or set of tools that produces mistakes. For example, they will frequently ask me, "Why not simply get rid of tests?" There are many situations where attempts to validate tests have proven unsuccessful. But many companies (too many, in my estimation) have thrown out all tests as a selection device because some were found to be faulty. Such a decision is tantamount to pitching out the "baby with the bath water"; tests are one source of information in a process where sources are not plentiful.

My point is that as a behavioral scientist, I would have to say that a perfect selection process is possible, but not probable. A more realistic objective is to have a selection process that minimizes wrong decisions and maximizes right decisions.

Grids are in vogue today. Here is one to illustrate:

Present Evaluation

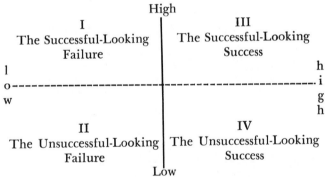

The diagram reflects four quadrants and four possibilities for hiring or promotion decisions.

The vertical scale represents the recruiter's or manager's present evaluation of the applicant (based on such sources as interviews, test scores, reference checks, biographical information). All points below the horizontal line, for example, represent people whom the decisionmaker judges unsuccessful.

The horizontal scale represents the measure of job

performance, *if* the applicant is given a chance to perform. All points to the left, for instance, represent people who will *perform* unsuccessfully on the job.

When the two lines are juxtaposed, four quadrants of the diagram are formed. Let's look at each:

Quadrant I: The Successful-Looking Failure.
This individual is commonly known as the flash in the pan. The evaluator is impressed, but once on the job, the person will fail. This is the first type of selection error.

Quadrant II: The Unsuccessful-Looking Failure.
This individual can expect the letter stating: "We have reviewed your qualifications and feel they do not match the objectives of our company at this time." The evaluator has done his job correctly: He has found the individual to be unsuccessful looking. His subsequent job performance is poor and supports the suspicion.

Quadrant III: The Successful-Looking Success.
Using such terms as "water walker" or "not yes, but heck, yes," the evaluator is correct in his findings: the person looks good, is good, will be good.

Quadrant IV: The Unsuccessful-Looking Success.
Here is another error in judgment. The evaluator sizes up the individual as a poor risk. In actuality, he's a sleeper, and if hired, would perform well. (If you would like some examples of this, I can guarantee a method for getting them: When you find yourself at a party and someone asks, "What line of work are you in?" tell him you are in personnel and you are thinking about using psychological tests as part of your selection procedure. After some initial comments about how intriguing such procedures are, he will tell you a series of stories about uncles and

fathers who scored low on supervisor's tests and later became company presidents or sales managers.)

In terms of the diagram, the objectives of your selection process should be to maximize the correct identification of failures (Quadrant II) and successes (Quadrant III), while minimizing mistakes made by hiring flash in the pans (Quadrant I) or by turning away sleepers (Quadrant IV).

The Role of the Interview

Any realistic approach must recognize that the interview is just one element in the hiring decision. Reference checks, background information, and possibly tests are all vital sources for decisionmaking.

Put another way, no one predictor, such as an interview, test score, single reference, or one piece of biographical information, should be used to determine whether the person is hired or not.

The most effective selection decision must be based on a systems approach. There are only a few predictors that a decisionmaker has at his disposal. He should not limit himself to one of these. Even organizations that use many different types of predictors (e.g., tests, interview, background data) have compiled the information in such a way as to put almost all of the weight on the interview. This was done by giving all of the test and background results to the interviewer and letting him make the final decision.

The systems approach has been advocated by the majority of selection specialists and by a panel of psychologists asked to make recommendations to the Equal Employment Opportunity Commission (EEOC) on fair selection. They wrote:

> We recommend the use of a *total personnel assessment system* toward the attainment of equal employment opportunities for all Americans. The many components of an objective personnel assessment system, i.e., job analysis, development of criterion-related validity, psychological testing, recruitment, screening of applicants, interviewing, and the integration of pertinent personnel data, provide the employer with the basis for matching manpower requirements with human aptitudes and abilities that are most likely to be nondiscriminatory within the spirit of the law. ("Guidelines on Employment Testing Procedures," EEOC, Aug. 24, 1966.)

Ignoring the systems approach is a fatal error. Interviewers can put too much emphasis on their interview impression. They feel this is the only available information. They assume they have a good knack for judging people. Their broad experience and perspective put them in the esteemed category of a good judge of horseflesh. But they're putting all their eggs in one basket.

The problem with such an approach can be crystalized by a true but extreme example. I was asked to participate in an interview board to award college scholarships to high school seniors. Six of us interviewed twelve candidates for four scholarships. Each student had excellent academic credentials. One member of the board sat through all the interviews and asked only one question of each candidate. "Were you a member of the Scouts?" When the board voted, I noticed that this gentleman rated all the ex-Scouts as "good" and non-Scouts as "less than good."

While membership in the Scouts is one benchmark, to consider it the only effective predictor of merit is a gross oversimplification. Some people may even consider it a negative indicator for some jobs. Whether positive or negative, this man had put all his eggs in one basket. He obviously had not read this book.

In sum, an ideal selection system is one which integrates all available avenues of information (including the interview, biographical information, references, and tests) to maximize the hits and minimize misses. One should always keep in mind that any selection system consistently used in business carries a certain amount of error. Rather than trying to eliminate all error, the company should aim for a program that reduces error. That's the real objective of a selection process.

chapter **2**

Guidelines for Sound Interviewing

Before we go on, let me caution you again:

Don't underestimate the importance of the interview. Talking is not interviewing, but effective interviewing is a sophisticated process and can be a valuable source of information.

Don't overestimate the importance of the interview. The interview is only one source of information about an applicant. It can be an imperfect source. Don't put all your eggs into this basket. Now, about the interview.

Find Out What You're Looking For

One day I received a call from a man who asked if I had a test for memory or recall. I told him I might be able to find one. I also asked him why he wanted such a test. The voice at the other end of the line explained that he was president of a small company and was hiring salesmen. Salesmen or sales candidates with the best memory turn out to be the best salesmen, he stated with authority.

I replied with an exclamation-pointed, question-marked "Oh!?"

The rationale for this, he continued, was that while a salesman was visiting a customer and looking around, he had to be able to remember what he saw and heard. Then he could come back to the office and tailor make a sales program based on his recollections.

Once again the eggs-in-one-basket syndrome. While memory may be helpful in sales activity, total reliance on this quality reflects limited knowledge about personal qualifications for a sales position.

Another real life example highlights a reverse problem. One of the nation's largest companies was seeking a railroad expediter at its headquarters. The manager felt this job was extremely important. Every job in his department was important. This vacancy could only be filled by a college graduate, in the top 10 percent of his class, who had had plant experience, was rated excellent, had high potential in the company, and needed "broadening experience in a challenging job like this." A friend of mine, who was substituting for the vacationing transfer and promotion personnel manager, swallowed this line. He sent out a request to the company's other locations for candidates. A few were submitted, but they proved totally unsatisfactory to that manager.

Around and around it went, until the veteran personnel man returned. He hired a retired railroad clerk with a high school education—who is still performing excellently on the job.

The attempt to hire people without a clear understanding of what you are looking for is one of the major difficulties in successful selection. Line managers are usually quite fuzzy in their own minds about the qualities they really want, except to say that the candidate should be intelligent, honest, and hard working.

Job Analysis

Drawing up a job description is the first step in job analysis. You must identify in detail all the responsibilities of the job and write down the personal specifications needed. What personal qualities does an individual need in order to get the job done?

These could include aptitudes like numerical ability, mechanical comprehension, creativity, and/or technical training (in specialized fields ranging from engineering to accounting).

What about personal qualities essential to successful execution of the job? Must the individual be hard driving? self-starting? a good planner? persistent?

What about interpersonal qualities? Does he have to be outgoing, able to relate well in unfamiliar groups? Must he be capable of accepting explicit rules and regulations? Can he work with supervisors? Can he direct the efforts of others?

Only after the personal specifications for a particular job have been listed should the interviewer begin his work.

Another useful exercise is to identify and list the *essential* specifications (musts) and then the *desirable* specifications (wants). Again, they should be exact and job related. For example, to specify that a sales-man must be pleasant is hardly satisfactory. To what kind of people must he relate on sales calls? Even within the same formal job category (securities sales-man, for example), one person may call on individual accounts while another may call on institutional accounts. Clients are different. The wrong kind of pleasantness with a particular group could be disastrous.

Personnel managers with large departments simply cannot develop solid specifications for a second shift foreman position in shipping and receiving without help. Suggestion: interview individuals who have held the job or who are now supervising it. This time used can certainly be justified to line managers on the ground that the more the personnel department knows about a position, the more effective it will be in getting the square plug for the square hole. (A form that can be used to record the job analysis is on Page 113.)

If you directly supervise the job in question, you need not do an in-depth job analysis. Obviously, you already know the job in an intimate way. However, you might want to talk to the peers of those who were not successful to get a more specific feeling for why previous jobholders had difficulty performing.

Some interviewers find themselves across the desk from a job candidate when they know little (and certainly less than is necessary) about the job in question. I would venture to guess, and it is just a guess, that more than 50 percent of the errors made in predicting job success based on the interview are due to the limited awareness of personal specifications need for a particular job.

The answer to this problem is adequate job analysis prior to the interview. The field of job analysis is extensive and there are a number of effective approaches. For further discussion of this topic, see *Industrial Psychology* by Milton Blum and James Naylor, "Content Validity: a procedural manual," a publication of the International Personnel Management Association.

Understanding the major procedures in job analysis is important. If you find yourself in a situation where you are asked to interview a job candidate and you are not sufficiently familiar with the job to conduct the interview, feel free to admit that you need specific information about what is being looked for. Many supervisors, executives, and personnel people hesitate to do this. They are concerned that they may appear less than knowledgeable about what is going on in the organization if they must ask questions about a specific job and its functions.

This is unfortunate because ignorance of job specifications contributes to the general fog surrounding the interview and prevents a clear understanding on the part of the candidate as to what qualities are being examined.

The trick in a successful job analysis is to make it job-related and behavioral. The necessary knowledge can be attained simply by asking those who are familiar with the job what specific tasks are performed.

When a person is asked about a specific task required for a particular job, he has a tendency to be general and vague (e.g., "Oh, what does a sales manager do?" "He supervises the salesmen and takes care of major accounts"). In order to appreciate the real demands of this job, the interviewer should ask the job expert (the person familiar with the job) to give specific examples of the more general statement. "Can you tell me something about the major accounts that the sales manager calls on and how he contacts them?" Or, "What does an electrician really do when you say he installs electrical systems in a domestic or industrial site?" The job description can be broken down into such things as working from blueprints that he must read, understanding what his supervisor tells him, co-ordinating his efforts with those of members of the other trades, and many other specific behaviors.

Another effective procedure in finding out more about the job is to ask people who are performing or supervising the job to think of people in the past who did not perform adequately. Be quick to point out that you are not looking for names but specific behaviors that they can pinpoint in order to explain why a person failed.

In some organizations, a job description of the position is helpful in getting a basic understanding of what is involved. However, many of these descriptions are inadequate and should be elaborated upon by talking to one or more incumbents or their supervisors. Some questions about the job should be asked of people familiar enough with it to identify the personal qualities necessary to execute the responsibilities adequately.

A book published by the United States government, *The Dictionary of Occupational Titles,* lists many job descriptions and may be helpful in giving you additional information about specific positions if you cannot find information elsewhere. Remember, avoid the danger of getting a biased view of the position requirements. Talk with more than one person doing the job, and talk with them individually when possible.

Preparation for Interviewing

The limited amount of time available to an interviewer dictates that that time be used as efficiently as possible. Conducting the interview without preparation is not unlike a surgeon entering the operating room before examining the necessary X-rays. Both procedures may be successful, in spite of the limited familiarity with the situation. But time will have been wasted and the inevitable groping may have caused unnecessary pain.

Before elaborating on this issue, let me say that I am not advocating arduous hours spent in reviewing applications or background information forms. I recognize the press of day-to-day activity and the resulting need to get on with the job. I am suggesting that an interviewer thoroughly acquaint himself with the specific personal specifications of the position before the interview begins. This can be done in a relatively short time. The interview conducted with foreknowledge will be far more valuable.

Interview Location

Where do you conduct interviews?

One basic tenet of sound interviewing is that an effective dialogue must be established. Two people (or more in group interviews) must be actively *participating*. Unfortunately, participation is often side-stepped when interviews are conducted in a setting that is physically antagonistic to good communication.

Department supervisors and managers are particularly negligent here. One company with a manufacturing plant in a large southern city had its first-line supervisor conduct interviews on the plant floor as the supervisor continued to perform his job.

A new job candidate has a difficult time focusing on the questions during an interview in such surroundings and he certainly would get the impression that he was not being considered seriously. However, the decision does not always lie with the department supervisors. At times, interview space is not available. In this case, management must be informed of the cost involved in failing to provide an adequate interviewing space: poor decisions and possible loss of good people.

Does a sound interviewing environment have to be plush? No, but it should be relatively quiet and free of distractions. Finally, the candidate should be able to talk without being overheard. Interviewees will generally feel more at ease if they believe their comments are being made to one person only.

Opening the Interview

We have already discussed the importance of the interviewer's preparation. An interview conducted on the spur of the moment or spontaneously is probably better than no interview at all, but it will not generate the rich quality of information that the well-planned interview will. I am always reluctant to use the term "well-planned" because this connotes hours of studying application forms and trying to phrase questions just right. On the contrary, I recommend a ten to fifteen minute systematic recap of a candidate's application form prior to the interview.

The objective simply is to form a general picture of the person and also give the interviewer an opportunity to react to any unusual elements in the candidate's background. In addition, there is a snowball-effect with unprepared interviewers. When the interviewer enters the situation unprepared, he begins thumbing through the application form, trying to catch up and read what he should have read before. In the process, he loses the information the candidate is giving and misses opportunities to follow up on important questions and subsequent answers.

Interviewer Attitude

The amount of information gleaned from an interview is directly related to the posture of the interviewer. Research conducted by a psychologist named Verplank, *Journal of Abnormal and Social Psychology*, 1955, demonstrated the interviewer's ability to influence the progress of the interview significantly by simple verbal statements. The interviewer's agreement in this situation would be implied by such reactions as "You're right," "I agree," or "That's so." Each interview was taped and analyzed for the number of statements of opinion made during the interview. Significant increases in statements of opinion were found during those interviews in which the interviewer followed expressed opinions with such statements of agreement as "You're right," "I agree," "That's so." More specifically, the interviewers in this study were instructed to respond to interviewee expressions of opinion in one of four ways:

1. Agreement.
2. Paraphrasing—the interviewer repeats the the interviewee's opinion statement.
3. Silence—the interviewer refrains from any comment immediately after the opinion.
4. Disagreement—the interviewer expresses

disagreement with every statement of opinion.

The agreement and paraphrasing interviews increased the frequency of opinion responses above the base rate (agreement was the more effective of the two). Disagreement and silence decreased the number of opinion statements below the base rate. In this regard, disagreement was more effective in reducing the number of opinion statements than silence was. Another psychologist, Greenspoon, independently arrived at similar findings (*American Journal of Psychology*, 1955). This study shows that the interviewer's behavior bears directly upon how the interviewee will perform.

Generally, we tend to feel more open and relaxed around people who are friendly to us. I have certainly observed this in the thousands of interviews that I have conducted. If the objective of the interview is to gather job-related information about the applicant, the probability of achieving that objective is enhanced by a friendly and personable attitude. It would improve the quality and quantity of this information if the examiner were able to communicate his honest regard for and interest in the interviewee. I'm obviously not talking about phoney, sugar-sweet, or artificial pleasantness toward candidates. On the contrary, I think there must be a conscious effort on the part of the interviewer to remember that each candidate is a person who has aspirations and wants to communicate his ideas in a positive manner.

While the interviewer cannot become too involved with any personal problems the interviewee brings up, he should not go to the other extreme of total insulation. There is practical reasoning behind this statement. A cold, distant, impersonal demeanor on the part of the interviewer will freeze the communication lines and limit the amount of information exchanged. Basically, there are three forces that operate on a person who interviews from day to day that, in turn, encourage rather impersonal interviewing posture. These are: (1) sheer numbers, (2) fear of being artificially personable and phoney, and (3) a related concern that being open and personable is not professional.

The first point needs little explanation for the experienced interviewer. A typical situation may arise when an interviewer has had anywhere from two to ten interviewees in one day. He must interview one more before he leaves for a board meeting with his superiors and the president of the company. Under such conditions, there is a strong desire to rush through the interview and get it over with before going on to the meeting.

If the examiner spends all of his time chatting about non job-related topics, such as the local football team's performance or the energy situation, time may be wasted because sufficient job-related information is not collected.

However, the examiner can be direct, to the point, and businesslike and still be open and pleasant. Such a posture will always generate information. The old attitude that the interviewer should be detached in order to make an objective judgment has been distorted. Some interpret it as an indicator that the interviewer should be cool, aloof, and above it all. There is an assumption that, if you are as cool and aloof as a computer, you will not influence the person's behavior. The only problem with this kind of assumption is that the person's aloofness influences the interviewee's behavior in such a way that it impedes communication, the basis for holding the interview.

There is a tendency to want to achieve a cold interviewer demeanor as a way of remaining constant and providing a standard selection condition for all candidates. An interviewer can retain just as much of a standard by being consistently open and personable as he can by being consistently aloof.

In opening the interview, you should put the person at ease by explaining what you are about and what your intentions are. Introducing yourself is a minimum requirement, as is telling the interviewee the purpose of the interview and informing him what positions are open. If he has a need to talk about non job-related topics, you might engage him in that activity for a brief period and then firmly move into the heart of the interview.

Begin the interview with a discussion of the candidate's work and/or scholastic record. This makes sense to the interviewee. It is preferable to discussing his childhood aspirations, for instance. An initial review of the job history serves to reduce some apprehension the interviewee may have about the employment interview.

We have already seen that an interviewee is sensitive to the subtle cues of the interviewer (Verplank, 1955). These cues should be used to encourage the interviewee to communicate openly and directly.

Let us assume you are interviewing a candidate for a first-line supervisory position and you want to see what type of attitudes he has about supervision. In this scenario, the candidate begins talking about a poor supervisor he had and contrasting him with a much better supervisor he once worked for. In this type of situation, the interviewer may obtain a great deal of information on the desired topic of attitudes toward supervision by actively responding to the above comments with verbal cues such as "I see," "I understand," or with a simple nod of the head. These phrases are just suggestions and can be easily replaced by the words with which the reader feels more familiar. After an interviewer has consciously made an effort to do this in a number of interviews, it becomes natural and fits easily into the interview.

This particular approach has two direct benefits. In addition to generating information on *your* topics, it reduces anxiety in the candidate by showing him that he is discussing information in which you are interested.

When the interviewee is communicating openly and answering the questions directly and candidly, these responses should be met with some slight encouragement by the examiner. This is also true when the interviewee discusses material relevant to the job description. The interviewee comes into the situation unsure of what is to be discussed or what the interviewer is interested in. Encouraging the interviewee to continue reduces some of the anxiety he has in not knowing what you want, thereby increasing the flow of information.

Let the Interviewee Do Most of the Talking

Daniels and Otis (*Personnel Psychology,* 1950) are two researchers who closely examined such specific aspects of the interview, as how much time of the total interview was taken up by interviewer talking, interviewee talking, and silence. Their analysis of numerous interviews have revealed 57 percent of the interview time (which is designed to gather information about the interviewee) is taken up by the interviewer's talking. Only 30 percent of that time is devoted to the interviewee's remarks and the remaining 13 percent is occupied by silence. These percentages communicate an even more severe problem of information-gathering when one realizes that many interviews last for less than ten minutes. If the interviewer were to follow all of the sound basic interviewing tactics except letting the interviewee do most of the talking, he would still have limited time in which to acquire the necessary information. Obviously, this is stacking the cards against the interviewer. Consequently, this business of allowing the interviewee to express himself is critical.

How do you encourage candidates to articulate their ideas? The general answer is to provide a friendly climate, one that is conducive to self-expression. More specifically, this means that you take action in three specific areas: (1) prepare for the interview, (2) spend a few minutes taking the edge off the candidate's apprehensions, and (3) ask questions in an open-ended manner.

There appears to be a powerful pull on the interviewer to talk rather than to structure the interview so as to get the interviewee to carry the ball. One of the qualities that frequently differentiates a good interviewer from a poor one is this area of communication. In the courses I have conducted, I have observed that the interviewer is somewhat uncomfortable unless he is saying something. This type of behavior cuts into the productivity of the interview and the amount of useful material obtained. This difficulty that interviewers have in maintaining a listening posture is one of the most troublesome problems.

One should not only focus on what a person says to you (content) but also on the way he says it (process). Two candidates may report that they have had difficulty with their previous supervisor. I suspect that each had a different type of problem or at least viewed his clash quite differently than the other, even though they both admitted difficulty.

Although few of us are psychoanalysts, a number of professionals in that field frequently speak of listening with a third ear to describe effective attention paid to what is going on in the interview. This includes body movements as well.

My intention is not to make analysts out of interviewers. However, there are obvious differences in interview behavior that should not go unnoticed. For example, if the interviewee is rather nervous and fidgety, and finds it difficult to answer questions directly in a concise, crisp manner, he should not be placed in a sales position where he must come up with answers to clients' questions quickly and intelligently. I raised an objection to relying overly on body language before. I still have reservations. However, this does not mean that one should ignore the postures and physical qualities. In fact, they may have some bearing on an individual's effectiveness on the job.

A person who sits in a chair wringing his hands throughout the interview and constantly articulating his ideas poorly may not be effective in a position requiring substantial social contact. But this should not automatically rule him out of consideration for jobs not requiring these social skills—a job such as a bookkeeper or research worker, for example.

On one occasion, I was interviewing a candidate for an office position. He arrived at the interview in tennis shoes and a shortsleeved shirt. He was slightly dirty. My initial reaction was negative. He pointed out that he had just come from work and began asking some rather unusual questions. This reinforced my negative reaction. However, when I was writing his report after the interview and later had a chance to review the test results, my evaluation was essentially at odds with the interview impression. As a result, I overruled my basic impression of the interview figuring it was simply my middle-class values and cultural residue that caused the negative reaction. Who was I to make a judgment that men who come to interviews should all wear ties and suits? I recommended the man for the job. Three weeks later his employer called me and told me that the man was a disruptive influence. So I really dropped the ball that time. The point is, while you should not totally rely on your first impression, the overall interview impression is a valid input into your total evaluation.

Of course, you can go too far in the other extreme and get to the point of the two psychiatrists who passed each other on the street one day. Their brief encounter was characterized by one saying, "Good morning, George," and the other thinking as he passed, "I wonder what he meant by that."

In determining whether some of the candidate's mannerisms or verbal communications are significant and require noting, one should try to relate it back to the job for which the person is being considered.

For example, if the person looks up at the ceiling when he answers questions, this may not be a problem for an office research position or accounting responsibility. However, it could obviously be a rather substantial impediment for a high level account executive position.

Structuring the Interview

On the one hand, the interviewer does not want to hand over the interview to the candidate so that he can talk about anything he would like and communicate little. But he does want the interviewee to speak spontaneously and thoughtfully to articulate his ideas along prescribed lines.

Trying to achieve a proper mix of spontaneity and structure is a worthwhile but elusive objective of a sound employment or promotion interview. My own view is that a completely structured interview in which the interviewer simply writes down the specific answers of the candidate to a set of predetermined questions is a waste of time. There is no reason why the interviewer should have to take his time to fill out the application form for the candidate.

The interview should be structured to the extent that specific areas are discussed (part performance in previous employment, reasons for leaving previous positions, reasons for wanting this position, related experience, educational background and preparation if relevant, etc.). The interview should not be concluded without getting the information in this area. What this information is should be predetermined to a large extent by the interviewer's efforts prior to the actual interview.

The information should be obtained by using

open-ended questions which will allow the candidate to respond in his own way. For example, an open-ended question such as, "What did you think of your last job?" usually generates a much richer response than asking "Did you like your last job?" Other examples of open-ended questions are, "Discuss your reasons for choosing this career. Why do you want this job?", etc.

Any given job interview will contain job-specific questions such as "Discuss the kinds of work you have done working with your hands?" (for electrician apprentice) and "What experience have you had working fifteen to twenty feet above ground?" (for a lineman position). However, there are a number of general qualities around which the interview can be structured. These include the candidate's ability to understand the examiner's questions, and secondly, the ability to articulate a response. Thirdly, can he relax in the interview situation? Or, is he so rigid that his comments are exclusively restricted to answers to the examiner's questions and nothing more?

I remember one nervous applicant who was trying to generate a sound impression but opened the interview by nervously spilling coffee all over my desk and papers. While this could happen to anyone, it fitted with the applicant's overall anxious demeanor. Another dimension is the interpersonal impact an individual has on others when first introduced. Although this is important for almost any position, it would be particularly so for sales and managerial posts.

The major values of structuring an interview are twofold: (1) a checklist is provided to cover each essential point (this is not a small asset); and (2) there is greater standardization of the interview procedure.

The results of a structured interview can be recorded on a patterned interview guide (see Appendix A) which not only covers the questions to be included but also provides space to rate a candidate on certain key qualities. There are many types of interview guides available and their objective is to include major factors or dimensions or qualities on which to rate an interviewee after the interview.

These guides can be used in a number of ways and should be selected only after some form of job analysis has been conducted. It is not uncommon for an interviewer to look at an interview guide before the interview and get the feeling that the form is totally useless in achieving the objective he has set for this interview. That's why many department managers and section supervisors use their own methods and their own forms to record information during an interview.

Here, I would have to say my colleagues in personnel are at fault. The form is sent out to all departments and in many cases it simply is not appropriate. In these situations, the user of the form has the option of throwing it away or striking out those qualities that he is not interested in for a particular position. One point that is frequently overlooked in this area is the ease with which a new form is devised. Such a patterned interview guide requires simply the identification of qualities in which the interviewer is interested and a five-point or seven-point scale that can be put right next to the quality. For example, if one is interested in determining the candidate's impact on others when he first meets them, he can simply list the quality, "Impact," on a sheet, possibly with a parenthetical definition of why impact is important on the job (e.g., candidate, as a sales manager, must communicate with vice presidents of manufacturing plus many top accounts throughout the country), with a five-point scale leading from one, below average, through three to five, above average.

If one wanted to be more thorough, he could generate a list of suggested questions to ask of the candidate under each of the qualities to be examined. These questions should be open-ended and nonleading in order to generate the maximum amount of information.

The basic point I am trying to get across here is the relative ease with which peer-made patterned interview guides can be developed for a specific position. I say relative ease because one of the most difficult aspects of developing these forms is not the identification of dimensions but the task of generating sound, nonleading, open-ended questions for each dimension.

Wrapping-Up

A mistake that can be quite harmful is the failure to close an interview effectively. It is not a common mistake but it creates problems. When the interviewer completes an interview, he should have resolved in the candidate's mind what is going to happen next. The interviewer does not have to indicate that a decision has been made, but he should familiarize the interviewee with the forces that are operating in the decision. For example, saying when the decision will be made, how it will be communicated to the candidate, and on what basis it will be made, or mentioning other job possibilities within the company if this particular job is not available. Indicate to the candidate what his chances are in getting the job. This doesn't mean the decision is made, but it does give an applicant some general idea of how many people are being considered. Such a conclusion is only common courtesy, but in the rush of day-to-day business, it is too often forgotten.

At the end of the interview, let me caution the professional interviewer to write down his reactions to the person right away, not ten minutes later, or the next day, but immediately afterward. I have been burnt on too many occasions when I have interviewed a person and later tried to remember and describe my feelings about him.

Some interviewers will see as many as ten or fifteen people per day, occasionally even more. To put off making comments about a particular candidate even until the noon hour is to lose a great deal of potential benefit simply because of procedural mistakes. It will take only a few minutes to sit down quietly and go over the answers to your questions and to assess flow of the interview on the whole. But it must be done immediately after the interview. A few minutes of time doing this is well spent.

Before moving away from suggestions on steps to be taken in an interview, consider the sound alternatives to the one-to-one situation such as the joint interview with two, three, or more persons talking with an applicant. This is particularly helpful when the interviewee has a limited amount of time. This topic is discussed in more detail in chapter 8 on future selection procedures.

One other comment that should be made about the joint interview. There are more meaningful outcomes when three independent opinions of a candidate's potential are given. In this case, three heads are better than one. However, always remember that the interview opinions should be independent. This means that the three interviewers should not discuss the results and impressions gained from the interview until each one has come to a decision individually.

chapter 3

How to Interpret Interview Data

On one evaluation that I wrote I suggested that the candidate might have limited drive and ambition. Among the facts that indicated this, I mentioned that the interviewee had left high school in his sophomore year. The owner of the company, a multi-millionaire, had terminated his formal education at seventh grade. Needless to say, he found my report, especially the comment about dropping out of school, amusing. While I had not implied that dropping out of school automatically meant limited drive, the situation my report created can be used to drive home an important message for any one interviewing and interpreting data collected.

There simply are no ironclad rules in successful interviewing. A person who has prospered in previ-

31

ous jobs will probably perform the duties of a new position effectively. However, this is not a certainty. He could well come in and perform miserably. In contrast, a person who has moved from job to job but without increased responsibility could conceivably come in and do a fantastic job in a new position.

The second, as well as the first, experience is unlikely but not impossible. A big mistake that some interviewers make is to generalize from one particular event. What does one do then, simply not attach much significance to any comments a person makes? Obviously not. But, instead of making generalizations based on limited information, the interviewer should begin a process of hunch building or hypothesis testing.

For example, if you have given a candidate a series of tests that show his intellectual skills are far above average, and yet you also notice that his performance was just average in high school and college, then you will likely entertain the notion that he is not especially ambitious. If you probe further by asking the candidate what kinds of activities he engaged in during undergraduate years and discovered that he worked thirty-five hours a week while taking eighteen hours a semester, you will modify your evaluation of his ambition and drive.

By contrast, if you discovered that this same individual didn't work during his university years or during the summer, then you would have additional support for your hypothesis of limited motivation and drive.

Let's get away from school and work and look at another example. Mr. Smith, a candidate for Corporate Controller, has come in for an interview. A review of his background indicates that he has held a number of jobs for fairly long periods of time and that he has had increased responsibilities on each job, until he became the number-two man in his department. However, this man is now fifty-five years old; he has still not attained the number-one slot in, let's say, the financial department. Following the process of building hunches, we now figure that Mr. Smith has a fear of becoming number one with all of the responsibilities and headaches that position entails.

We could further entertain the hunch that he does not possess the initiative and self-starting quality required to be the top person. There are many such people who are quite effective and contribute a great deal when given specific direction but who cannot provide the initiative or tolerate the final responsibility for running an entire department. Checking references may throw some light on this subject but additional information can also be obtained through the interview. This is an excellent opportunity to confront the candidate with your hunch.

Do not fall into the trap of being worried that this will offend the candidate or make him feel bad. It is more unfair to the candidate if you do not share your hunch with him and give him an opportunity to respond. For example, you could say, "I notice that on each job you have risen in responsibilities but have not gone beyond the number-two position in your department. Can you tell me why this pattern has developed?"

The interviewer is faced with a dilemma. On one hand, the question must be asked or the interview is worthless. On the other hand, one of the major weaknesses is the interviewer's tendency to form a hasty conclusion about the candidate during the first few minutes of the interview and spend the rest of the time looking for information to verify that snap reaction. This initial impression may be inaccurately perpetuated by the interviewer's reluctance to discuss any sensitive issues. It is more unfair to the applicant to omit a question about an issue that is troubling the interviewer (e.g., Why have you had four jobs in the last three years?) than to sweep it under the rug without giving the applicant a chance to explain.

The interviewer must be aware of this problem and attempt to handle it. Hopefully he can develop a willingness to resist snap judgements combined with a readiness to probe for more information. For example, if the applicant reports that he quit school at the tenth grade, the interviewer should resist the temptation to conclude automatically that he is either immature or intellectually slow. At this point, the interviewer should probe the circumstances surrounding that decision. Possibly, the candidate's father died and he had no alternative but to go to work. Perhaps he subsequently obtained a graduate equivalency degree. Once a question has been thoroughly probed, and only after it has been thoroughly probed, should a hunch be accepted or rejected.

Accuracy of Interview Information

The business of accuracy frequently haunts interviewers. "Is this person really telling me the truth?" is a question that often runs through the interviewer's mind. Certainly, all candidates want to put their best foot forward. How much distortion does this lead to? A study conducted by three researchers, Keating,

Patterson, and Stone (1950), checked on the accuracy of information given during the interview. They concluded that over 90 percent of the information given during interviews was essentially correct. This included such details as salary, duration of past employment, and duties. Slightly poorer agreement was obtained by Weiss and Dawis (1960) in a study of ninety-one physically handicapped persons. These results tend to contradict the uncomfortable feeling that many interviewers experience, namely, that much of the information that they are getting is false.

Along these same lines, it is suggested that the interviewer ask the candidate to describe himself. Years ago, behavioral scientists felt that the best way to identify the real person under all the socially acceptable masks he wore was to give inkblot tests and/or ask indirect questions. However, our society is more open and direct now. From the behavioral sicentists, we have a more rational concept of man. And so today we confront candidates more directly. One question I have found helpful and informative is "Given duties and responsibilities of this position, what do you consider your three major strengths?" Once this question has been answered, ask the person to list any weaknesses he might experience if he were operating in this position.

One study on college students (Worell, 1959) attempted to predict those who would be successful in college and those who would not. The researchers used high school grades, test scores, and many other predictors. None of these predicted success effectively. Finally, someone suggested that the students be asked themselves to predict how successful they might be. This self-analysis turned out to be an effective predictor of how well an individual would do in college. In other words, students who said they would do well by and large did better than those who had some reservations and were concerned about their college performance. To speculate why this was true would be interesting, but more important is the fact that a person's own ideas and feelings are strong indications of the actual outcome. In addition, there is a certain amount of logic to the idea that the person who is most familiar with the candidate's performance is the candidate himself.

Let me say a word about nervousness during the interview. Some interviewers unfortunately assume that simply because a person is uncomfortable and nervous during the interview he will react similarly on the job itself. This assumption may or may not be true, but one should at least consider the possibility that a job interview is a particularly anxiety-provoking situation for many people and that these individuals will probably be much more relaxed on the job.

I have already made a comment about the interpretation of schooling, but, obviously, one should examine a person's professional and academic training. While it is legitimate to consider early school termination as one indicator of immaturity or limited ambition, the emphasis should be put on the fact that it is just *one* indicator and, as such, could be false. If you observe other factors that seem to point in the same direction, then you may support your hunch more strongly.

Job stability, or length of service with a given employer, is another quality frequently considered admirable and desirable, particularly if the person has moved up within the organization. Moving from one job to another is neither as damaging nor as indicative of instability as it once was. Our society has changed to the point where there are many competent people who may have held two, three, or possibly even four, different positions within a ten-year period. This is particularly true in some industries and types of work, such as data processing, and of some personnel like key punch operators and programmers.

It is also useful to examine whether or not job changes constitute a step upward. Obviously, such examination should be tempered with a knowledge of the general economic conditions. A few years ago, there were a number of competent people being relieved of their jobs simply because of mergers or recession. Many of these people did not obtain new positions for a long time, and some who did get other jobs had to take less pay than they received before. Obviously, the meaning attached to this type of job change would be quite different than to job changes under more normal circumstances. This is another time when it becomes imperative for the interviewer to share his views and concerns about a job-seeker's track record with the person himself. If this is not done in a situation where the candidate has had numerous jobs, the interviewer may falsely conclude that the frequent job changes were indicative of a personality problem when, in point of fact, there may have been legitimate explanations for many, if not all, of the job changes.

Another area to probe is the candidate's type of military experience. If he has not had this experience, it may be useful to find out why. Obviously, if a man had experience as a welder in the army and is applying for a similar position, the interviewer should have this information. It may also be important to recognize if the candidate went into the military service as an enlisted man and increased his rank and areas of responsibility during his tour of duty. Such information may lead to quite a different hunch than the fact that the candidate was discharged at the same rank as he had when he entered the service.

Giving the Interviewee Information

Up to this point, we have explored questioning the job applicant. However, another function of the interview is to provide the candidate with information about the organization. The interviewer should describe the position in question accurately and candidly. If the objective of the interview is to get the best person for the job, certainly a partially informed job candidate is not the best prospect.

Let me give you an example. One industrial firm had a high turnover rate in one category of job. The position required hard work, in 90° F temperatures, and occasionally handling dangerous chemicals. Dissatisfaction was causing high turnover which in turn lowered morale in the department.

The manager then instigated a tour through the plant for all serious candidates, explaining the specifics about hours, discomfort, and so forth. The result was a dramatic reduction in turnover among new employees. The case illustrates an important point. The more an applicant knows about the job at the beginning, particularly the negative aspects, the less friction he will experience later. If I am told in the beginning that cleaning up the work area every third week is part of my job, I will be much more willing to accept this as a normal requirement. But, if I am told three weeks after I'm on the job, I may feel that I have been taken advantage of. Time familiarizing the new or prospective employee with his duties is well spent.

Most interviewers use a series of questions that they feel are quite helpful in getting the necessary information. Toward the end of the interview, it's inevitable that the candidate will desire to present some information which has not been discussed. When one job applicant was given this opportunity, he told the examiner he did not want to nor would he travel more than 25 percent of his work time. This was useful information because the position required more than 50 percent travel time. Other candidates will use this opportunity to describe why they want the job and to reiterate why they think they can do it. In some cases, a candidate doesn't want to bring up unsolicited information, but in other cases, he might be quite willing to share additional facts if given the opportunity. Frequently, information is lost because there is no specific question that gives the candidate an opportunity to bring it up.

Consequently, I recommend that one of the closing questions given to the candidate be a broad, open-ended question regarding information not previously discussed that might be important for the interviewer to know. Such a question could be phrased a number of ways, such as, "If you have anything to add regarding you and the job, please feel free to bring it up now," or, "Take a few minutes while I review my notes and try to think of additional information you may want to bring up about you and this job."

Since this type of question can imply that the interviewer is looking for something in particular, he then should qualify the question by saying that he is not looking for anything specific. In addition to possibly providing some fruitful and informative facts about the candidate, such a question also gives the interviewee an opportunity to add anything not covered during the more structured part of the interview.

This type of question has a number of benefits. A major one is that it relieves some anxiety in the applicant by giving him an opportunity to say whatever he has on his mind. I also recommend that the interviewer ask the interviewee if he has any questions. This courtesy is all too often overlooked.

The interviewer can also suggest that the interviewee mentally review topics covered in the interview and add any relevant, additional points after thinking about it for a few moments. You can also tell him exactly what you are going to do during that time, namely, review your notes to see if there is anything that you have missed. Obviously, it is much better to discover any point you may not have covered before the person leaves. Take two or three minutes and systematically and thoroughly review what data you have gathered during the interview and ask any other questions you subsequently think of before closing the interview.

The candidate may ask about his particular chances for the job or say, "What do you think, how did I do?" Such questions should be handled honestly at the time even though most interviewers don't know what the overall reaction to the interviewee has been. I often have to sit down for a few minutes after an interview and gather my thoughts. I would freely tell the candidate as much as I could about the number of positions available and how long the company is planning to interview, as well as when the candidate will be notified. If you have planned the interview well and determined what qualities and personal specifications you are after, the chances of ending the interview before you have obtained all of the necessary information will be reduced dramatically.

In this chapter I have included sample reports that will provide you with some impression of the final product stemming from the interview. It should be pointed out that these are samples only and the reader should feel free to improve on them.

At the end of this chapter, I have sketched four sample evaluations of interview data. In them, I suggest using a 1-5 numerical rating to judge job-related qualities. This format is relatively unusual for evaluations of interview data, but it has two distinct advantages over other approaches: (1) It forces the interviewer to focus on specific job related qualities, thereby straightening out his thinking along job-related lines. This minimizes much of the fog usually surrounding the results of an interview so indicated by the phrase "my overall gut reaction to the candidate was bad," or "I got positive vibes." (2) Forcing oneself to review all the data accumulated on one quality and then evaluating it by assigning a number from 1, very poor, to 5, very good, results in a more exact and specific evaluation of the interviewer's reaction to the interviewee's behavior. Relatedly, it allows for more precise communication among those discussing the candidate's qualifications.

This is *not* pigeonholing people. Labeling a person's overall work qualities such as, "he's a 5," or "she's a real comer," as the sum and substance of the interview results is not only unappealing but also counterproductive. It blurs meaningful distinctions such as "being very assertive and hard working and productive when working by himself and asserting himself in dealing with others."

It is quite a different thing to say John is a 2 than to say the interviewer's impression of John's level of ambition is 2 and list specific reasons for making that judgment.

In the following samples of interview reports, notice the attempt to use both background information and interview data to describe specific and job-related factors (e.g., ambition, drive, intelligence). Each of these factors are rated on a five-point (Likert) scale— 1 means the person did not impress the interviewer in a particular area, 3 is just average, and 5 indicates that the candidate was high on that factor.

1	2	3	4	5
Low	Below-Average	Average	Above-Average	High

Evaluation A: Position in Question: Plant Manager
1. Biographical Sketch

(This section contains some of the more pertinent events in the candidate's background.)

Statistical Information
Date of Birth: July 17, 1935
Married; three children

Educational Background

1958	Purdue University B.S. in mechanical engineering
1970	University of Illinois M.B.A. in management
1964	Attended courses at Pittsburgh University Law School; took courses in communications at Allegheny College

Employment Record

1959	U.S. Army; Corporal
1959-1960	Johns-Manville Corporation, Chicago Position: sales manager
1961-1962	U.S. Army; Sergeant
1960-1965	Textron—Talon Division, Meadville, Pennsylvania Position: Design and project engineer
1965-Present	Hobart Brothers, Troy, Ohio Positions Held: manager of manufacturing; plant manager (most recent)

2. *Biographical Comment and Interview Impression: Intelligence and Learning Ability:* 4 Mr. Rhone has displayed his intellectual ability at both Purdue University and Illinois. The engineering and the business degrees will be of help to him in the plant manager position at Topper Plastics.

Drive: 3 He has displayed a capactiy to work for a company over a long period of time as well as increase his responsibilities as a result of his on-the-job efforts. He spoke positively of his experience with his present employer and indicated that he would not be considering a position at Topper Plastics except for his son's deafness and the facilities here at St. Joseph's School for the Deaf.

Oral Communications: 4 During the interview, Mr. Rhone impressed the examiner as being a bright person and one who could articulate his ideas in an efficient manner.

Impact: 3 He related to the examiner in a fairly personable way but generated a feeling that he was above all "this selection business." As a result, he acted somewhat the prima donna, with a suspicious air about him. These qualities should not be over-emphasized and, in general, Mr. Rhone made a fairly positive impression.

Evaluation B: Position in Question: Assistant to the Controller

1. Biographical Sketch

    (This section contains some of the more pertinent events in the candidate's background.)

    Statistical Information

    Date of Birth: May 5, 1946
    Marital status: Single

    Educational Background

    1968   University of Kansas, B.A. in finance;
           Grade point average: 3.1 in 4-point system
    1972   University of California,
           M.B.A. in finance

    Employment Record

    1956-67   Communications Telephone Company

Summers Position: Business Representative
1968   Communications Telephone Company
Summer   Position: Manager/Business Office
1968-70   U.S. Army
1970-71   Communications Telephone Company
           Position: Commercial Staff Assistant
           (part-time)

2. *Biographical Comment and Interview Impression: Ambition:* 4 Although Mr. Gorman's work record is not very long, he has demonstrated both a willingness and capacity to move forward in any objective he sets for himself. This was evidenced by his getting a M.B.A. with a B+ average. He has also shown a spirit of adventure by taking paratrooper training during his military service. That same spirit motivated him to seek employment with a relatively new firm in an attempt to "get in on the bottom floor."

Impact: 4 The impression he gave was also quite positive, reflecting the capacity to articulate his ideas easily and to listen attentively. He had no difficulty understanding the examiner's questions and generated the impression of a man who was self-confident and enthusiastic about his work and his ability to make a contribution to that work.

Experience: 2 The only factor in Mr. Gorman's background that can be interpreted as negative is his simple lack of experience. He is obviously planning to correct this.

(Note: Many of the above hunches about the candidate's intelligence were confirmed by subsequent testing.)

Evaluation C: Position in Question: Productive Manager

1. Biographical Sketch

(This section contains some of the more pertinent events in the candidate's background.)

Statistical Information

Date of Birth: May 11, 1923
Married July 3, 1949; two children, ages 19 and 16

Educational Background

1942-43	University of Illinois,
1946-48	B.S. degree in engineering
1948-50	Wayne University Graduate School business administration major

Employment Record

1943-45	U.S. Air Force
1948-52	Ford Motor Company
1952-55	Box, Eileen & Hamilton—management consultant
1955-58	Cutlass-Wright
1965-68	Tryco Position: general manager
1968-73	Borg Warner Corporation: M-S Div. Position: works manager
1973——	Boring Carburetor Division of MGH Industries, Incorporated Position: production manager Reason for leaving: compensation and benefit package less than expected

2. *Biographical Comment and Interview Impression: Ambition:* 4 Mr. Curt's educational back-

ground and achievements are impressive in quality, as well as quantity. Not only did he earn his engineering degree from the University of Illinois, which should be of obvious benefit in a manufacturing company, but he also graduated in the upper quarter of his class. Subsequently, he went through pilot training and demonstrated his leadership by commanding a squadron during World War II.

Flexibility: 4 Mr. Curt has also shown flexibility in his work as a consultant and has dealt with top management on a day-to-day basis. In addition, his work experience shows that he is capable of managing a large manufacturing unit. This was displayed at Boring Carburetor as well as previous positions he held.

Job Stability: 3 The only concern his background generates is the fact that he has held a number of positions for three or four years of duration only. When confronted with this employment pattern, Mr. Curt answered that many of these changes, if not all of them, were quite legitimate and some were precipitated by the organization (such as Borg Warner's move to Toledo).

Impact: 4 The interview impression was quite positive and Mr. Curt generated a sound impact on the examiner. He was articulate, logical, and apparently forthright.

Ambition: 4 Mr. Curt finds himself in a situation at Boring Carburetor that prevents him from capitalizing on his past and present contributions to the profit picture at Boring. He wants very much to be in a position where performance has a dollar incentive. It is a fact that Boring has gone through some top-level changes in the past and that part of his story can be substantiated.

Oral Communications: 3 The only weakness in the interview impression was a slight tendency for Mr. Curt to stall or periodically break his train of thought in the middle of a sentence. This is a slight irritant and takes away from his overall positive impact.

These interview impressions were supplemented by test results that identified Mr. Curt as a very bright person with superior analytical skills, numerical ability, and reading comprehension.

Evaluation D: Position in Question: Administrative Assistant to the President

1. Biographical Sketch

(This section contains some of the more pertinent events in the candidate's background.)

Statistical Information

Date of Birth: May 2, 1943
Married: three daughters

Educational Background

St. Catherine's Academy, graduated among the top ten of her class

Employment Record

1961-1962   Worked part time during senior year—three nights per week and on Saturday
1962-Present Olympia Electrical Products
     1965   Executive secretary to incoming president of Works Right Division
     1971   Secretary to Chief Financial Officer of Olympia

1972   Supervisor of Corporate Accounting
       Clerical Functions
1973   Administrative Assistant to Chief
       Financial Officer

2. *Biographical Comment and Interview Impression: Job Stability:* 5   Ms. Brokaw's work record is impressive and entirely with one specific employer. The fact that she worked her senior year in high school indicates some drive and willingness to apply herself in order to achieve her objectives. Her employment with one firm for the past twelve years is an obvious indicator of job stability and suggests that a change from one company to another at this time is rather unlikely. This is reinforced by her interview comments which indicated a good deal of satisfaction with her present job.

Initiative: 5   The fact that she has increased her responsibilities over the years suggests an effective use of her work skills. More specifically, these positions have required the ability to handle special projects on her own and see that they are achieved. Her history of promotion is indicative of substantial initiative.

Oral Communication: 4   During the interview, Ms. Brokaw displayed an ability to express her ideas in an articulate and concise manner. She was personable and did not appear to hide any information about her working past. She also appeared to be able to listen effectively and understand the examiner's questions with little difficulty.

Impact: 3   The only negative trait that appeared in the interview was a tendency for Ms. Brokaw to appear slightly more uncomfortable than most people do in a psychological evaluation. Part of this may have been due to the fact that there was some confusion as to which office she was to come to. However, the examiner believes that some of it was due to a slight amount of uncertainty about herself. This was reinforced when she was asked to list two accomplishments of which she was most proud. Ms. Brokaw could only think of one and that was, "a pretty good job of coordinating things at Olympia." In spite of this one weakness, the overall impression was still positive.

chapter 4

Validity—Fair Employment and the Interview

What can and cannot be asked in the interview?

I have discussed some of the basic tools for and findings about effective interviewing. But I can almost hear some of my readers out there saying, "That's fine, but in today's market you have governmental agencies who tell you what you can and cannot ask in an employment or promotional interview."

In this chapter, I examine governmental guidelines for interviewing in today's marketplace.

One basic principle is that questions asked should be job-related (i.e., Have you had previous experience in this type of work?).

A corollary of this rule has been seen in many recent court cases. More specifically, any selection process that rejects a higher percentage of a group protected by the Civil Rights Acts of 1964 and 1972, than the percentage of the mainstream of society would come under scrutiny to determine job-relatedness of that procedure. In fact, the employer who finds himself with such a selection procedure could then be required to demonstrate its job-relatedness. The question, "Have you ever been arrested?" on the surface appears to be job-related, but in the state of New Jersey, for example, it is illegal to ask that question. Why? More blacks have been arrested and in some cases this is done as part of a mass roundup of young blacks. The potential employer *can* ask, "Have you ever been convicted?" This question gets at the heart of the issue without unduly penalizing the black applicant.

A few states, such as New Jersey, have lists of illegal questions. It should be noted that these questions are not illegal in all situations but their content will give the reader some idea of possible objections to some interview questions.

Questions that ask an applicant about membership in specific organizations are considered to be a contrivance to establish ethnic or political ties (e.g., Black Panthers, National Organization of Women, The Young Americans for Freedom). Membership in these groups may give insight into the candidate's attitude toward certain political issues but have little to do with his ability to do the job.

Obvious questions about race, religious affiliation, or ethnic origins are frequently illegal, if not, in poor taste. This is also true of such related procedures as having pre-employment photographs taken. Such a practice was not uncommon in a number of companies and involved photographing every applicant who reached the point past the screening interview. The candidate's picture would accompany his file through the channels of selection. The legitimacy was to recall the person in the minds of those making the selection decision. However, it was an obvious opportunity for some selectors to automatically rule out members of protected groups.

Department managers should be generally sensitive to these issues in conducting selection and promotional interviews. However, having familiarized themselves with these caveats they should not be frozen into inaction by fear of asking a sensitive question. On the contrary, interviewers should continue to conduct a sound, factual, and honest session using the suggestions made earlier.

Specific rules about these sensitive areas will change from time to time according to different court cases. There is no list etched in stone. However, two principles will not readily change and should be kept in mind: (1) Is the question job-related? (2) Does it disproportionately "select out" minorities?

Keeping this in mind, an interviewer should be able to conduct his interviews enthusiastically and freely. I choose the word "freely" because I have seen many department and personnel managers become concerned at the prospect of interviewing a minority member, and sometimes a woman.

This leads to unnecessary anxiety and undue concern. Two negative effects are possible: (1) the interviewee is uncomfortable because you are uncomfortable; or (2) the interviewee preceives your uneasiness and will try to use it to get the job (e.g., "I was not going to apply here because your company has the reputation of being discriminatory."). Such a comment could be a legitimate concern of the individual or a pressure point applied to you in your uneasiness.

The above problems can be reduced if one keeps the two principles in mind, prepares for the interview, and asks questions in the same manner that he would use for other candidates.

The final point in this chapter has been a source of concern among interview experts for years—"the Structured vs. Non-structured" controversy. This topic will be discussed more fully in chapter 6, but it is important to mention here because it deals directly with a practical facet of the everyday interview and its effectiveness as a selection tool.

One of the most compelling attractions of the interview as a tool of selection is its capacity to afford the selector an opportunity to get a first hand impression, allowing him to look and talk to the candidate. This generally comes under the topic of "getting to know the candidate."

There's certainly nothing wrong with that. The problem comes when one realizes that different interviewers "get to know" the applicants in quite different ways. One may do it by using a stress oriented technique (i.e., a stress interview involves asking the candidate stress generating questions, such as, "You have had three jobs in the last four years. Can't you keep a job?" or, "Are you always as nervous as you are in this interview?") If another interviewer interviews the same candidate in a personable and supportive manner, he may perform quite differently.

In many organizations, selection and promotion

interviews are conducted by one interviewer on Monday and another interviewer on Tuesday with possibly a third doing the interviewing on Wednesday, Thursday, and Friday. Under such conditions, disagreement between interviewers who have independently interviewed the same candidate is not only possible but frequent. This lack of consistency between interviewers (lack of Inter-Interviewer Reliability—IIR) may cause one of a pair of equally qualified people to get a job because he had an easy interviewer while the other had a tough one.

One of the appeals of objective tests is that they can be administered in a standardized manner (every test taker is exposed to essentially the same experiences).

So, that's the problem and there are no total solutions. One proposed solution has been to standardize the interview by requiring the interviewers to ask the exact same questions in the exact same sequence and write down the applicant's verbatim reply. This process would certainly generate a higher degree of standardization, although there would still be the problem of differences in the abilities of individual interviewers to transcribe the candidate's remarks.

Even if one could eliminate all of these inconsistencies between interviewers and have a completely structured interview, those who question the structured interview would ask, "Why have an interviewer at all?" In most cases, the candidate can read the questions and write his own answers.

The point is that the richness of the interview information is to a great part due to the interviewer's option to follow up on responses which may suggest additional questions and further probing. The structured interview form does not have this advantage.

My own opinion is that a certain amount of structure maintaining some standardization is good. But this should be accompanied by a built in flexibility which allows interviewers to follow up promising responses. This can involve a patterned interview guide, like the model in Appendix A, or a slightly more sophisticated approach of having a pool (group) of sound, open-ended questions from which the interviewer could choose.

This approach would minimize the probability of a future candidate gaining knowledge of the questions before the interview. Another advantage of this question pool approach is that it allows the interviewer some latitude in choosing questions with which he is most comfortable. The questions in the item pools are grouped according to the quality on which they are designed to shed some information (i.e., a pool of questions would be generated for ambition, another pool generated for interpersonal assertiveness, another pool for ability to plan and organize, etc.).

One additional step can increase IIR. Your staff of interviewers could participate in a well-designed, intensive, and experiential training program in which they do actual interviewing and watch themselves on video tape. This would allow them an opportunity not only to become more familiar with the pitfalls commonly associated with the interview but also to receive immediate feedback regarding areas in which *their* own interviewing techniques need improving. Such a procedure should be helpful in improving both the skills of the individual interviewer and the IIR of your entire interviewing staff.

chapter 5

The Counseling Interview

Little has been written about the counseling interview. However, there is constant demand for supervisors to counsel their employees regarding their work performance. In all too many cases, supervisors finding themselves with a subordinate who is not doing his job either sit around and wring their hands about the problem or take the posture that the problem will correct itself. While I can appreciate giving the subordinate an opportunity to work things out for himself, I also recognize the importance of taking some constructive action once it is clear that the subordinate is not effective in dealing with the problem.

A discussion between a supervisor and a subordinate about a work problem is called an Employment Counseling Interview (ECI). When a supervisor plans an ECI, he frequently becomes concerned about being too assertive and domineering when he discusses the subordinate's poor performance. An even less effective approach is for a supervisor to become so passive that he doesn't get any ideas across in the ECI.

A counseling interview should be guided by the following five points:

    1. Review work requirements or objectives of the subordinate, and how they relate to the group's requirements or objectives.

    2. Emphasize that it is the subordinate's responsibility to accomplish his objectives and tie these to the group's objectives.

    3. Point out *specifically* (using examples) how the subordinate's performance has been unsatisfactory.

    4. Obtain the subordinate's solution and conduct a dialogue on the efficacy of that solution, telling subordinate's solution. Here the technique discussed in previous chapters of the book (probing, using open-ended questions, directing the interview, etc.) should be applied.

    5. Record date of talk; and in serious problems, obtain signed, dated forms stating that the supervisor and subordinate have talked and agreed to a solution. If agreement cannot be reached, obtain signed and dated statements that you have talked and discussed the topic. The form should be so worded that the supervisor's stated solution is acknowledged, if not agreed to, by the subordinate.

How would such a form work? Let us take a look at a few examples. However, realize that use of such a form is optional. The supervisor should decide whether it is appropriate in his work group.

Situation: Over a week's time, an order filler in a warehouse has been more than a half hour late on three occasions. The supervisor is uncomfortable with this situation because orders have been backing up in this person's area. Some supervisors would have some qualms about even mentioning the tardiness to the subordinate.

It is unfair to both the subordinate and to the organization to allow the situation to continue unchecked. The ECI can be a brief five to ten minute conversation or an hour discussion, depending on the situation and the judgment of the supervisor.

In this case, it could result in a relatively short discussion beginning with the supervisor pointing out the objective of the order filling department and the supervisor's current problem.

HANK (supervisor):   Jason, in this department we have the job of getting out the orders. We are supposed to get them out right and to get them out fast. I'm responsible, and I don't feel that we are getting our job done.

You have been doing fine for the last eight months, but during this last week you have been late three different times. Not only has that disrupted your area, but the other order filler's work has backed up making the problem bigger. What has been going on with you this week?

JASON: Well, Hank, I've had car trouble. My car wouldn't run because the radiator is broken. I tried a sealant, but it broke down on me Monday, overheated on the freeway on the way to work, and made me late. I have had to take the bus the last four days, and twice the bus has been late.

HANK: Well, what do you think we can do from here on in to get you to work on time?

JASON: This weekend I am going to try and pick up a radiator out of an old wreck. My car isn't worth a new radiator. If that works, I'll be here on time.

HANK: And if it doesn't?

JASON: I don't know, I guess I'll have to take the bus again.

HANK: But it got here late twice this week.

JASON: Well, I guess I am going to have to catch the earlier bus and get here a half hour before work starts.

HANK: It might even be a good idea to start out earlier if you drive. Those used parts work sometimes and then other times they don't. Jason, let's leave it at this, but I do want you to know that it is important that I get my job done and to do that, you have to be here on time. I am going to sign a statement that we discussed this problem today and I want you to sign it too. Do you have any questions?

JASON: Yeah, what's this form about?

HANK: It is simply a form for my records that we discussed this problem on this date.

JASON: OK, let me sign it.
(Note—Usually a subordinate will sign. If he does not, note his refusal on the form and have someone else witness that you did hold the discussion on that date and put it in the file.)

Performance Discussion Form

                                    Date: February 25,
Employee's Name: Jason Hargrove
Supervisor's Name: Hank Schwartz
Major points of discussion: Reasons behind the employee's coming in twenty minutes late on three separate occasions were discussed. It was agreed that broken automobile would be repaired or an earlier bus would be taken to assure subsequent arrival at work on time.

                    Employee _____
                    Supervisor _____

   The five steps to be covered are basic points and do not have to be the only ones addressed in the ECI. Conducting the interview should be a smooth flowing and natural experience, but bringing the interview off may take some practice on the supervisor's part. The more comfortable he is with it, the less uncomfortable the subordinate is going to be.
   Let's take a little more subtle and perhaps more difficult situation.
Situation: Joe Miller, a male subordinate, has been critical of almost every program Rachel King, his female supervisor, has recommended and implemented in her data processing department. He is not as critical of others in the department. Joe's performance has not been up to par and Rachel is

beginning to observe a similar hypercriticalness in some of Joe's friends who also work in the data processing department. Joe sat through several rehearsals of a presentation to be given to the "big Boss." He said nothing, but he thought, "the proposed new program *might* work, if we're lucky." When the presentation was actually being made by Rachel and several of his peers, Joe "sandbagged" them. He was disruptive, pointed out problems not relevant to the new program, and asked specific questions of Rachel, which she could not possibly answer. Everyone was embarrassed, including the boss. Following the meeting, the boss vacillated in his decision that the new program was worthwhile. Rachel had to visit him personally later and resell the program.

An ECI between Rachel and Joe should stress the major objective of the department. It should also clarify that Rachel intends to give the job her best effort.

RACHEL: Joe, I have been reviewing our department's performance over the past three months. Overall I feel we have done a good job. I walked into some major problems when I became data processing supervisor. But the entire department has worked together to correct many of these problems.

However, I think that we can do even better. There's one area in which you can really help. Over the past month and a half, you have been quite critical of my recommendations. In four separate group meetings, you have leveled your criticisms but you have failed to come up with alternative suggestions. I don't want "yes" people around me, but I would like criticism to be constructive.

JOE: I don't know what you're talking about.

RACHEL: We met with the accounting department two weeks ago about the new payroll procedure. Even though our department and most of the accounting department agreed on my suggested approach, you claimed it was unworkable even though you sat in our department meeting earlier and gave no criticism of it.

You made no suggestions in the joint meeting regarding a better solution. I want to work with you, but there seems to be something bothering you and I would like to give you an opportunity to talk about it.

JOE: I did have some reservations about your suggestions that I hadn't thought of before. But there is nothing bothering me.

RACHEL: I would encourage you to be critical of programs that you feel are not doing the job, but go farther and come up with some alternatives. You're a programmer and closer to developing and revising programs than other members of the department. You have some ideas of what will work better. Bring those to my attention and I'll try to do something about them. Is there anything else you wanted to discuss?

JOE: Since you have been frank with me, I will

tell you that I make my suggestions because I believe your programs reflect your limited experience in the programming field. You haven't worked in that area and can't be expected to know. I do think that your lack of experience prevents you from being a well-rounded data processing supervisor.

RACHEL: Well, management has examined my record and decided that I do have the qualifications to be the supervisor. I am going to try and justify that confidence as much as I can. I can appreciate your point of view. I am not too familiar with some of the program languages that are required in some of the specific projects at the company. That's why I need the support of someone in the programming department. I need someone I can depend on for advice. I would like that to be you.

JOE: I don't have any hang-ups about giving you advice, and that is what I have been trying to do.

RACHEL: Well, I appreciate it, Joe, but I would prefer your giving it to me in our own internal departmental meetings. When you identify problem areas in our proposed programs, try to come up with a suggested alternative.

JOE: I thought I had been doing that, but I will try and focus more on my remedies to the problems.

RACHEL: Don't overlook the problem. Obviously that's important also. If you get anything on these new program languages that you think I could assimilate, send them my way. I'll see that you get the information back.

By the way, will you handle the shipping and receiving project presentation coming up in two weeks? I'll give you all the help I can. You will be presenting it to the Director-Data Systems in our next semi-monthly meeting.

Performance Discussion Form

Date: December 12, 1974
Employee's Name: Joe Miller
Supervisor's Name: Rachel King
Major points of discussion: Method of making suggestions by the employee was discussed. The supervisor emphasized the importance of suggestions but pointed out the critical nature of the suggestions being made by the employee. The employee indicated his feeling that these suggestions were given in a positive vein. There was agreement between the employee and the supervisor regarding an increased effort to provide alternative suggestions when criticisms are leveled.

Employee _____
Supervisor _____

The basic function of the work group supervised by a single supervisor and its whole reason for existing are to accomplish a basic organizational objective. This could be production, control, shipping, research, finance, or whatever. That basic function and its objective should be held central and reemphasized repeatedly during the ECI. This is the first and most essential of the three concepts to keep in mind while conducting a counseling interview.

Far from using the interview to beat the subordinate over the head with a problem, a supervisor should focus on business objectives. For example, "Our department has a problem in meeting its work objectives." "Can you tell me how you perceive the difficulties in this area?" "What would you recommend as a solution?" This method gives the subordinate an opportunity to tell his side of the story and also requires that subordinate to come up with a solution. This technique is known as putting the monkey on the subordinate's back. If he comes up with a sound solution, put it into effect. That person will be highly committed to making it work because it was his own idea.

As soon as possible after an acceptable trial period, establish a follow-up date to review the effectiveness of the recommended solution.

If the solution is working, the subordinate should be complimented for the idea. If it is not working, he should still have the ability and willingness to come up with another potentially sound idea. Next, modifications of the solution should be worked out and another check-point set. It is important that these dates be established firmly and explicitly.

If the subordinate's original solution is without merit, he should become familiar with the problems it would create. The subordinate may disagree with the supervisor, but he must not abdicate his responsibility as a leader. After describing the problems one particular solution might create, the supervisor should thank that person for making a suggestion and encourage him to make other suggestions in the future. Present your solution and inform him that you want this solution implemented until a better one can be devised.

The advantage of mutual review of the subordinate's work and development of objectives by supervisor and subordinate has been recognized by George Odiorne. He has thoroughly explored these advantages and developed a detailed program for these review sessions. His program, Management by Objectives (MBO), has achieved widespread recognition; and one of the reasons is because it acknowledges the subordinate's need to contribute his ideas in developing an inviting work climate.

However, the program is mentioned here because it has a hard-nosed philosophy which also stresses the responsibility of the subordinate to come up with practical and effective solutions, as well as to identify problems. Many supervisors fall into the trap of devoting 100 percent of their time to the solving of the problems their subordinates uncover. This frequently stems from a misguided belief that their entire job responsibility is exclusively to shield their subordinates from the pains of solving any problems, thereby permitting them to work as efficiently as possible. This attitude toward subordinates is not unlike that held by many parents toward their children.

Unfortunately, such a paternalistic or maternalistic attitude causes resentment in many subordinates, the same way it would if the reader's boss treated him that way. At work, a supervisor should not be a parent, but a director.

The counseling interview focuses on three major considerations, always keeping the first point in central focus throughout the interview. The points are:

(1) the whole purpose of the supervisor and subordinate being on the job is to achieve our department's objective; (2) the supervisor's job is to organize his subordinate's efforts in such a way as to achieve that objective in the most effective and workable manner. A related point here is the supervisor is the one who will be held responsible (not the subordinate) if the department objectives are not achieved; (3) for some reason (tardiness, disagreement with other subordinates, etc.), the subordinate's work performance is not acceptable.

Perhaps this appears a little too much like a textbook solution, but let me assure you failure to recognize one or more of these points causes a high percentage of the problems in Employment Counseling Interviews throughout the country. Most discussions of the counseling interview stress the importance of really listening to the subordinate. I would underscore that point and advocate that a sincere effort be made, not only to fully attend to the subordinate's problem, but to cooperate with him in an effort to implement a solution.

The most effective manner for a supervisor to deal with these problems is to have a "business centered sensitivity." Such a sensitivity does not preclude changing in the manner of doing business if a better solution can be identified. There are a number of distinct and significant advantages to adopting this sensitivity and keeping the previous three points (i.e., department objective, supervisor's responsibility for department objectives, and employee's current failure to achieve these objectives,) in central focus throughout each Employment Counseling Interview.

The basic five step approach reduces guilt feelings

on the part of the supervisor. One of the biggest problems involved in the implementation of ECI's or the failure to conduct an ECI is the supervisor's apprehension about being too harsh or appearing to be too harsh. Following this procedure allows the supervisor to recognize the business necessity and purpose of the interview, thereby maintaining a perspective which minimizes any guilt feelings associated with the interview.

The approach allows the supervisor to treat the subordinate as an adult. The subordinate's ideas are explored and the results of his suggestions are discussed. Everyone feels there has been a fair hearing. In point of fact, the subordinate may come up with a better way to do the work.

The approach allows the supervisor to treat the into personalities." Because the interview's focus is on business realities and facts in the day-to-day situation, there is a minimum of counterproductive and nonspecific comments, such as, "You're always doing something wrong," or, "You're never doing things the way you should be," or, "You're never where you should be," or, "You always seem to make the wrong decision." If these generalizations are made without substantiation, they do not instruct and they frequently alienate.

While one should compliment and encourage the subordinate's positive activities, many supervisors and managers suffer a reluctance to tell it like it is in dealing with subordinates. This reluctance is a shirking of the supervisor's responsibility, and its negative impact is no more apparent than in the termination of unsatisfactory employees. On many occasions, I have been told that a particular subordinate has filed a complaint because he was dismissed without cause.

The reluctance to give feedback about the subordinate's work performance, whether it is good or bad, is one of the big stumbling blocks of effective working relationships in organizational life today. Although there are many evidences of this reluctance to give a subordinate feedback, the extreme situation makes the point more dramatic. In those cases involving a subordinate petitioning for a review of his dismissal, the subordinate's continuation has frequently been upheld. When one examines why this has happened in those cases, most of the time it's a failure to *document* and *inform* the subordinate of his performance problem.

At the time of the dismissal, a supervisor finds himself in a position of claiming a subordinate performed poorly but of not being able to back up the claim with facts. It then becomes his or her word against the subordinate's. So what does a supervisor do about it? I recommend first the conducting of counseling interviews in the manner previously discussed in this chapter. If a person is performing poorly, he has a right to know. Secondly, I recommend making it a practice of developing a dated form reflecting the fact that the specific problems the subordinate was having were discussed citing specifics (e.g., number of days late, etc.), and providing a place for the subordinate's and supervisor's signatures. If the supervisor does this with every ECI and puts the form in the employee's folder, it will not seem so out of the ordinary to the subordinate. But it does let the subordinate know that the discussion and specific facts have been recorded.

Positive feedback by supervisors is far too rare, also. This appears to be rather unusual, but one of the most substantial criticisms that subordinates have about their supervisors when given the chance to respond on anonymous and standardized attitude surveys is, "My boss rarely tells me when I'm doing a good job."

Research in the behavioral sciences has demonstrated the impact of positive reward on performance. (*Business Week,* December, 1971). But management has not used it efficiently to increase subordinate performance.

On balance, attitude surveys of hourly employees frequently identify positive feedbacks from employee's supervisors on the job as inadequate in more than 50 percent of those surveyed. That does not mean that you fail to signal poor performance to the appropriate party. You can do this by realistically and authentically acknowledging some good points about his performance but then pointing out the discrepancy between the objectives and the actual performance. Without dwelling on the problem, encourage your subordinate to achieve the objective the next time around and, also encourage him to let you know if there are some other problems.

Treat the subordinate as you would wish to be treated; but do not kid yourself, this kind of supervision is hard work. It is easier just to tell a subordinate to do something than to explain why. In the short run, it is easier to make the supervisory decision without discussing it with subordinates. However, you will be building a more effective subordinate and a stronger department if you involve him in these discussions. One of the differences between a poor or average supervisor and an outstanding one is the ability to see the interchangeability of the words "fish" and "work" in the following:

> Give a man a fish and you feed him for a day. Teach him how to fish and you feed him for a lifetime.

If you really instruct and encourage a subordinate to a point at which he can assume more responsibility, not only is he going to accomplish more for you, he is going to respect you. On the other hand, if you treat the subordinate like a mindless tool, he will measure up to your expectations and attempt to achieve no more than that.

The Exit Interview

When an employee has decided to resign, a company can learn a great deal by finding out the real reason for his decision. This is particularly true if the company is experiencing a drain of competent people as a result of resignations.

The exit interview, conducted by a company representative, is designed to determine the former employee's real reasons for resigning. The major problem in such an interview is generating sufficient candor on the part of the interviewee.

The interviewee may be currently looking for another job and does not want to rock the boat. He gives some socially acceptable and noncandid reason for his decision because he does not wish to run the risk of getting a poor reference from his former employer or supervisor. In some cases, the interviewer can convince the interviewee to be candid by honestly telling him that his reply will not affect his references one way or the other. But this is problematic because one is never sure whether the replies given under the above conditions are candid.

There is no absolute solution to this problem but I have used one method that can generate this candor after the employee has left. The solution also makes basic common sense.

Candor can be developed in the exit interview by conducting it after the former employee has his next job. In the security of that position, he has little if anything to fear in being honest in his replies. A letter can even be sent particularly if the new job is out of town. Follow-up phone calls will usually result in getting even the procrastinating former employee to reply.

chapter 6

Evaluating Your Interview and the Fair Employment Movement

Does your interview select the best candidates for the job and eliminate those who are less qualified? If it does, then your interview is considered valid. If it does not, then it is considered invalid. The intention here is not to explore the concept of validity in all its technical ramifications. However, it makes good sense to see if a particular selection procedure is actually identifying the proper people for the positions in an organization.

The business sense of establishing the validity of your selection procedure (validating) has been heightened by the generation of legislation in the federal government, such as the 1964 Civil Rights Act as amended by the 1972 Civil Rights Act. These acts plus Executive Order 11246 have made it clear that both private and public employers must take affirmative action in weeding out any invalid selection or recruiting tool. There are literally thousands of fair employment cases in which cities, states, unions, large corporations, universities, and many other types of employers have been brought to court because of an invalid selection, recruiting procedure. More specifics about these cases may be found in a series of volumes, *Fair Employment Practice Cases,* published by the Bureau of National Affairs.

Two specific cases will be used here to drive home pertinent points. These are the AT&T case and the *Griggs* v. *Duke Power* case. Essentially, the legislation mentioned above has generated two major federal commissions charged with issuing guidelines to employers and overseeing their adherence to these guidelines. The two commissions are the Equal Employment Opportunity Commission (EEOC) and the Office of Federal Contracts Compliance (OFCC). If a job candidate feels that he was not given a job because of his age, sex, or race, he has the legal right to file a complaint. The appropriate commission will investigate the complaint to determine its legitimacy. At that point, it can be thrown out or the employer can take steps to remedy a bonafide weakness such as an invalid selection tool in their hiring and promotional procedures. In some cases involving class action suits in which an employee represents a class of people who have been discriminated against (all female employees or all black employees in the company), compensation for past selection practices to those suffering from them have been granted by the court. Such monetary settlements can range from small amounts up to $46 million, awarded by AT&T in their consent decree.

While I hope that many organizations would validate or identify the effectiveness of their selection procedures, simply because it means good business, a number of employers have needed the additional and real incentive of the potential monetary loss resulting from a court case. The other fair employment case is not important because of its large dollar settlement, but because it involved the United States Supreme Court and the whole issue of testing. The Equal Employment Opportunity Commission considers the scorable interview as a form of test.

Basically, the facts were that the Duke Power Company was using a series of tests, as well as some educational requirements—high school graduation—in selecting employees for entry level jobs. The black employees were scoring lower on these tests than the white employees were. As a result, the work force had a much higher percentage of white employees than those found in the surrounding geographical area from which the work force was selected. The selection procedure was taken to court as being discriminating and invalid.

When the Duke Power Company could not come up with sufficient evidence to demonstrate the validity of its tests and high school educational requirement, the Supreme Court unanimously ruled in favor of Mr. Griggs.

Three basic points should be gleaned from this land-mark decision.

1. The highest court in the land said that an organization's selection procedure must be valid.

2. The decision in *Griggs* v. *Duke Power* was *not* a decision against testing or the employer's right to have and use methods to select quality people. Chief Justice Berger emphasized this in the following excerpt from his decision in this case:

> Nothing in the [Civil Rights] act precludes the use of testing or measuring procedures; obviously, they are useful. What Congress has forbidden is giving these devices controlling force unless they are demonstrably a reasonable measure of job performance. Congress has not commanded that the less qualified be preferred over the better qualified simply because of minority origins. Far from disparaging job qualifications as such, Congress has made qualifications to control factors so that race, religion, nationality, and sex become irrelevant. What Congress has commanded is that any test used must measure the person for the job and not the person in the abstract. (*Fair Employment Practices Cases,* Volume 6.)

3. The final important factor to be gleaned here can be labeled "the shift of burden phenomenon." Once it has been demonstrated that a selection, recruiting procedure has resulted in a higher percentage of the unprotected classes (e.g., white males) than of the protected classes (blacks, females, and older employees), then the burden of proof shifts to the employer. He must demonstrate the validity of his selection procedures or modify those procedures.

The results of all of this activity are twofold. First, there has been a substantial interest on the part of personnel managers and executives about fair employment procedures. "What does the EEOC want us to do?" is a frequent question clients have asked me. A second consequence has been a tendency for many employers to drop all testing procedures. In many cases, this is appropriate because the tests were not being used properly. In other words, the tests were valid but the company operated under the erroneous assumption that if they got rid of all tests, they wouldn't have any fair employment problems. Nothing could be farther from the truth.

For example, one organization hired clerical people by using an I.Q. test. Even if the gross generalization "smarter clerks are better clerks" were true (I have seen many people of average intelligence who have outperformed their more mentally gifted peers in a variety of jobs), there is the whole question of how tests of I.Q. actually measure intelligence equally from people of different races and age groups.

However, in too many cases, the employer pitches the tests before he determines whether or not they are valid (O'Leary, *Personnel Journal,* 1972).

To get a better grasp of exactly what the regulating agencies are asking, let's go back to my original diagram, found in chapter 1.

As mentioned, the objective of any selection program is to minimize errors and maximize successful predictions. It seeks to identify and hire the successful-looking *and* unsuccessful-looking successes. A committee selected by the EEOC with a blue-ribbon panel of psychologists examined this selection area and made a number of recommendations. One was to use a systems approach to selection. This approach advocates the utilization of all possible predictors before making a decision about hiring or promotion. Four possible sources of information are interviews, test results, background information (frequently referred to as bio-data) and references.

When companies make decisions to drop testing programs, they unwittingly eliminate one source of information. In addition to reducing their predictive success probability, they put an initial strain on the other three sources of information. Not a great deal of work has been done in the research area on references. However, I will attempt to demonstrate how the remaining two sources of information can be quite helpful.

There are two ways one can try to understand the governmental regulations. First, go through a list of don'ts and, if you aren't committing errors on this list, you can have some feeling of security. However, this can be dangerous because it may be that the agency assumes that everyone knows that particular practice is not permissible. Consequently, I believe it's better to understand the basic underlying principles behind the regulations and go from there.

The principles of federal employment legislation, as well as state and municipal laws, are fairly simple and direct. In one word, the objective is *validity*. "Validity" is a term which has a specific meaning in psychological and psychometric language. An employment test is valid if it predicts job success. If high scorers on a test do no better than low scorers when it comes to job performance, then the test is invalid and should not be used. Fair employment regulations include scorable interviews as a "test." A scorable interview is simply one in which the interviewer quantifies his impressions of the interview. I would hasten to add that this does not mean that unscorable interviews (these are interviews in which there is no effort made to quantify the results of the interview) are permissible or are more acceptable by EEOC than scorable ones. In fact, this is one of the dangers of simply reading a list.

Because the scorable interview can be quantified, it is possible to determine whether or not people who appear competent actually do better than those who appear less so. No such comparison is possible with the unscorable interview. It is next to impossible to validate the unscored or unquantified interview. However, with the increased pressure on the interview aspect of the selection program, there will be a substantial pressure to validate it. As a result, it will not be too far in the distant future when companies will be asked to demonstrate the validity of their interview procedures. Those companies using unscorable interview forms will find it impossible to produce such information.

I should add an additional point of extreme importance. A report, entitled "Labor Turnover Handbook 1970," (released by Merchants and Manufacturer's Association) gives the results of a survey in the Los Angeles area which indicates that the average cost of turnover of office and technical personnel is about $1,139 per person. It was also found that a valid testing program at Southern California Gas Company, which accepts 50 percent of the applicants, reduced termination rates for typing clerks by 36 percent.

If we take a conservative estimate of a company

hiring 100 people a year, they will save 36 percent of $113,900, or $41,006 a year; and this is a small company. If the employer is hiring 1,000 people a year, the estimated annual savings on turnover costs would be close to a half million dollars.

This savings does not even consider the increased productivity stemming from increased morale and worker performance, as well as a more stable work force.

Another company had a turnover rate in their plant operation of almost 95 percent in one year. Their total plant work force was approximately 500 people. If we were to say that this cost per hire was only $1,000, you will quickly see that the turnover cost alone for that company was something next to a half million dollars a year. That is a conservative estimate. Obviously, many organizations don't have that kind of turnover problem.

If you validate and update your selection system, you are essentially minimizing errors and thereby reducing your selection costs, training expenses, and so forth. In this sense, at times I feel like telling my clients, "The hell with EEOC . . . validate the tests for the same reasons you would check the efficiency of new EDP equipment or a new carrier for your merchandise. Validate it to see if you are getting your dollar value for your selection effort."

How to Validate

Although the interview is the most frequently used selection tool, relatively little has been done to evaluate its effectiveness in its validation. Lynn Ulrich and D. Trumbo (*Psychological Bulletin,* 1965) made a substantial review of the literature in this area and found that attempts to validate the interview were ineffective. There was no consistency in information gained by interviewing. In other words, some interviewers would ask certain questions and others would ask different information. This led to a lack of interviewer reliability or consistency.

This is one of the strongest arguments for having at least some structured aspects of the interview. The interviewer should use an interview work sheet which possesses a list of the qualities or personal specifications required for the job. Therefore, the first step in developing a quantifiable or scorable interview form is to identify as specifically as possible what characteristics are needed for a particular job.

These factors should be observable whenever possible. In other words, it would be difficult to obtain a measure of such a quality as creativity in a standard interview. You may be able to deduce something about an individual's creative ability, but it is not something ordinarily or consistently observable.

In contrast, such qualities as spontaneity or the ability to relate to people in a self-confident manner can be observed to a certain extent. You would then use a rating scale of 1 through 5 or 7 on that particular dimension. Finally, the interviewer should give an overall rating based on his impressions regarding the possibility of a candidate's success on the job.

You then simply go about your normal, day-to-day activity of interviewing and filling out these scored interview forms. After a sufficient quantity has been completed and certain people have been hired, some type of performance measure must be developed.

When possible, this can be an objective measure such as who sold the most business (marketing), who produced the most productive ideas (R & D), who produced the most equipment, material, or finished goods (production), and so forth. However, objective measures are frequently not available and one will have to rely upon supervisor ratings. There is a whole technique to obtaining sound ratings and minimizing subjective biases inherent in these ratings. One can find these kinds of techniques in industrial psychology books or bring in a consultant for that purpose.

The ultimate objective of a validity study is to determine to what extent the people rated highly during the interview actually performed well on the job. This can be accomplished through a statistical technique called a correlation. If the correlation between interview impression and job performance is sufficiently high, you have successfully validated your interview form.

Although correlation coefficients work much better with larger numbers, let's assume you have just ten employees in a given job and you can score the interview results and also have an accurate job performance score on each of the ten. There is a simple statistical procedure which allows you to see the degree to which higher interview scores perform better on the job than people who obtained lower interview scores. If the correlation coefficient is large enough, the interview is considered valid. However, the table below is just an example and one should not justify his selection procedure on this without talking to someone knowledgeable in the field of selection and statistics.

Employment Interview and
Job Performance Scores for Ten Employees

Name	Interview Score	Performance Rating Score
John	16	5
Mary	27	7
Jane	37	8
Odell	13	5
Foster	26	6
Jeff	12	4
Bonnie	35	6
Connie	14	6
Larry	36	10
Barb	11	4

These two columns of numbers can be easily combined in a straightforward formula to generate a correlation reflecting the amount and direction of the relationship between the two factors.

What frequently happens is that some parts of the interview form will not be valid (e.g., interviewer's perception of how forceful the candidate is may not be correlated with on-the-job success). However, other elements of the scored interview blank may be predictive (e.g., overall impression of the candidate's chances for success). Again, it should be emphasized that this is important information to possess. If you are basing your selection on impressions that really do not predict success, then you are using a selection device that is, at least partially, malfunctioning. The next step then is to weed out those nonpredictive factors.

What other research findings are there in the interview? Having personally conducted over 1,000 selection and promotional interviews, observed others conducting interviews (in their employment setting or interviewer training programs that I have run), and familiarized myself with much of the research on the interview, I have come to three major conclusions.

1. The selection interview is enjoying widespread use in selection and promotional decisions today. Spriegel and James (1958) surveyed 852 firms and found that 99 percent reported interviewing applicants before hiring. In an independent article, Bellows and Estep (1954) estimated that 150 million selection interviews take place annually in this country.

2. Efforts made to investigate whether the interview is doing its job (actually selecting the most qualified people for the job) is relatively meager when one looks at its widespread use.

3. In spite of the limited amount of research, there are some conclusions that can be drawn regarding the interview. A second major problem in addition to the limited amount of research is what I wish to call "the delivery system problem." There is no question that additional research is sorely needed and essential if we are to enhance our *knowledge* about maximally utilizing interview time in promotional and hire decisions. However, there should be an effort to communicate the practical results of past research to the decisionmakers who are daily conducting employment interviews on which they base a critical decision.

What are some of these findings? People who work in different levels of various organizations frequently find themselves evaluating the effectiveness of their physical equipment and of their services or products. Unfortunately, they are not as analytical in their evaluation of such selection procedures as the interview. In 1949, a systematic review of the published studies on the selection interview was conducted by R. Wagner. "A number of conclusions came out of that review, in which I surveyed 106 different reports on the interview. One of the major conclusions was that only twenty-five studies provided any quantitative evidence." Wagner felt that many of these twenty-five studies had substantial problems in the way they were conducted.

A subsequent review by Lynn Ulrich and Don Trumbo was conducted in 1965. A few of the major research findings covered by this review are rather informative, and they substantiate the number of techniques recommended in this volume.

Most of the research reported here will deal with studies that indicated certain kinds of interviews were successful. This is to accentuate and underscore productive aspects of the interview. Many studies which reported negative results on the interview are not included here.

In 1957, L. R. Bonneau conducted an evaluation designed to test the efficiency of the interview for predicting teacher ability to establish rapport with students. The results were impressive, indicating the interview's capacity to effectively predict the above skill. Unfortunately, this interview was quite unlike most employment interviews insofar as the interviewers were essentially data collectors only, obtaining categorical answers to eighteen pretested questions. However, it does indicate the importance of a certain amount of structure and consistency in establishing an interview format for an organization.

In another study involving an interview, A.

Trankell (1959) attempted to evaluate the potential of a number of predictors including a selection interview. The job that was being predicted was a training program for a pilot training course of a Scandinavian airline. Predictions were made on the basis of eight different traits deemed necessary for success in the training program. Five of these traits had been measured by using tests. Not only did the interview help in predicting the three remaining traits, but it also increased the predictive effectiveness for the other five traits beyond that achieved by the test scores alone.

This is the kind of result which substantiates the logical conclusion that one should know what he is trying to predict and specifically focus on those traits before he begins developing his interview plan. Another reason for introducing a certain level of structure in the interview is to establish reliability or consistency as a predictive measure. When a test is published, I must present information on how consistent the test is. This need for consistency is apparent in a test that would lack it. For example, how valuable would an I.Q. test be that measured your intelligence today at 106, tomorrow at 145, and the following day at 78? This need for reliability is real. But research on the interview has indicated some questionable levels of reliability or consistency. Part of this is due to the lack of structure which results in some interviewers having a completely different picture of what they are looking for in an interview than is found in the heads of other interviewers. In Wagner's (1949) review, there were 96 different traits evaluated but only twenty-nine had estimates of reliability of these measures.

One method of measuring reliability is to obtain two independent measures of a specific trait on each person interviewed. This is accomplished simply by giving the same interview worksheet to a number of different interviewers and having them independently complete the worksheet. Once these ratings have been completed on a large number of candidates for the same job (more than thirty-five or forty), a correlation coefficient can be computed (Sample Interviewer Worksheet, Appendix C).

This can be done even if a combined interview (an interview with more than one interviewer) is performed. You simply instruct the interviewers to complete their rating forms before discussing the candidate. Although there are some problems with a combined interview, namely the risk of intimidating the interviewee, it is my opinion that there are many benefits which have gone unnoticed and are associated with the combined interview. Most obvious among these benefits is the fact that the interviewee can answer the questions once rather than go over the same ground two, three, four, or even five times in five sequential interviews. One wonders how accurate a picture of a candidate an interviewer gets when that applicant answers the same question for the fifth time within a few hours. A second advantage is the cross fertilization of questions and ideas occurring between interviewers when a combined interview is conducted. Finally, all of the scheduling and rescheduling of interviews throughout the day can be reduced as well as the rescheduling required if one interviewer has to switch his interview time around. With the combined interview, either you attend the one interview period, or you do not.

Which type of information most dramatically affects interviewer opinions of the candidate? B. F. Bolster and B. M. Springbett (1961) attempted to evaluate this question by providing interviewers with protocols containing combinations of statements scaled for favorableness and unfavorableness. The results showed that negative information more readily induced shifts in ratings than did positive data.

Ulrich and Trumbo conclude their review of the interview studies by suggesting, "the results rather consistently indicate two areas which both contribute heavily to interviewer decisions and show greatest evidence of validity. These two areas of assessment may be described roughly as personal relations and motivation to work. In other words, perhaps the interviewer should seek information on two questions: (1) What is the applicant's motivation to work? and (2) Will he adjust to the social context of his job?"

I agree with the reviewers, but I further emphasize the importance of focusing on a specific and yet limited number of other variables or traits that could be measured by the interview.

chapter 7

Background Information

Past performance is one of the more effective predictors of future performance. This maxim is probably one of the underpinnings of the wide use of the application form and references before employers make a decision to hire. However, do you know what kind of background predicts success for most of the people and jobs in your company? You, of course, need available data on your present employees before you answer that question.

Many companies have the data in file cabinets, but it is not *available*. To get a real answer to "What kind of background is characteristic of people who have been successful in a specific job in my company?" you should examine the background of a large number of your employees. However, few executives have time to pull out old personnel files to figure out a common thread in the background of successful employees. Even if they did have the time, it would be a substantial cost in terms of executive time and the result may be only partially rewarding.

There is a better way that is thorough, systematic, and relatively inexpensive. It is usually referred to as a bio-data approach and involves systematically recording background information (e.g., application form information and additional data which the applicant provides) when the applicant applied for the job. Examples of this format are included below. When you look at the format, the important thing to note is it permits someone to come along and code the information into punch card data, which in turn allows the computer, not the executive, to do the work and to do it thoroughly.

Sample of Bio-Data Format

A. How long have you lived where you now live?
    a. less than 1 year
    b. 1 to 2 years
    c. 3 to 4 years
    d. 5 to 6 years
    e. 7 to 8 years
    f. 9 to 10 years
    g. 11 or more years

B. In which of the following courses have you had the most training?
    a. agriculture
    b. architecture
    c. biological sciences
    d. business administration

e. economics
f. education
g. engineering
h. English or literature
i. fine arts
j. foreign language
k. journalism
l. mathematics
m. music
n. physical education
o. physical science
p. psychology or philosophy
q. religion
r. social science
s. speech
t. sports
u. trade or technical
v. other (please specify)

C. In which of the following clubs, societies, or activities did you participate while in school? (Check as many as apply.)
a. dramatics, debating, or speech club
b. fraternity or social group
c. music, band, chorus, or orchestra
d. history or foreign language club
e. mathematics or science
f. literary magazine or newspaper
g. varsity sport
h. intermural sport
i. student government
j. other (please specify)

E. What was the product you dealt with on your most recent job?

a. had no previous job
b. service
c. metal or metal products
d. petroleum
e. foodstuffs or beverages
f. clothing or fabrics
g. building materials
h. home or farm equipment
i. agricultural products
j. electrical equipment
k. other (please specify)

A wealth of information exists in every company's file cabinet that could be used to predict success, but it is frequently not available. A number of major corporations, including Standard Oil of New Jersey, General Electric, and others, have successfully implemented systems that enable them to retrieve this kind of information easily. This approach does not require terribly complex or involved data blanks.

What does it require? Basically, a retrievable set of bio-data information requires a bio-data format that can be quantified easily. The reader should realize that this is different from a scorable interview and deals only with written responses on a specialized application (bio-data) form. This approach to selection has been quite effective in predicting turnover but it can also predict success on the job.

Rather than having a candidate come in and fill out an application blank in the traditional form, he is simply asked to fill out a bio-data form that asks essentially the same questions but in a multiple-choice format. Obviously, a number of questions such as work history do not lend themselves to this format and they will have to be included in the traditional form. However, if you evaluate your current application form critically, I think you will see that a substantial amount can be transferred to a multiple-choice format, such as the one above.

Two points about this procedure should be remembered: (1) No decisions to hire or promote should be made using this method until it has been proven valid. This would require a brief consulting time by someone knowledgeable in this method. (2) Usually, the bio-data format starts out with 100 or more items like the ones mentioned above. These are usually pared down to fifteen to twenty-five that prove effective for a specific job in a specific company.

The use of such a format enables a clerical person to take off the scores on the form and transfer them to a one-sheet page. Once you have the person's background information you can collect data systematically. The effectiveness in predicting turnover, job performance, accident proneness, and other work qualities will become easy.

While most application questions can be asked in a multiple-choice format, some will not lend themselves to such an approach. One of these is the usual request to list previous employers. But even here, you can design a multiple-choice question to use in addition to such a listing. Such a question could be, "How many jobs have you had in the last five years?" or, "How many years have you worked in our company's area of business?" These questions would also render some interesting information. The alternative answers could be one, two, three, and four, and alternative five would be "More than four." In addition to the standard questions, you could have an additional multiple-choice format that would ask questions not included as part of the hire decision but collected for research purposes only. In this section, you could ask such questions as number of brothers and sisters, age at marriage, favorite subjects in high school or college, and so on. The total number of questions might approach or even exceed 100.

After a sufficient number of such bio-data questionnaires were collected and some criterion of performance assessed with the same people in sufficient numbers, a statistical test could be run on the data. Such a test would identify which ones and how many items on the original bio-data form were answered in a significantly different way by people who stayed with the organization as opposed to those people who left and those were were rated well above average versus those who were rated below average.

Out of 100 items, you can usually expect to obtain anywhere between fourteen to twenty-five questions that would differentiate between two groups screened. These fourteen to twenty-five items would then be administered to your new hires on a routine basis and these questionnaires would be given a score. For example, if a new hire answered a given item in the same way that many of the turnover people did in a previous sample, answers to such questions would be given a negative value, such as −1. On the other hand, if that same person answered another question in the same manner that most long tenured people answered on a previous sample, that item would be given a +1 value. In this way, the questionnaire could be scored, and each bio-data form could be given a final score.

Again, these scores should be collected over a period of time until a sufficient number of cases are collected with either performance ratings or a turnover criterion. Once this has been accomplished, a simple correlation could be computed between these sample scores and the criteria, whatever it may be. If this correlation were significant (beyond the .05 level of significance), you would now have a valid selection instrument in the form of these fourteen to twenty-five questions.

There are many advantages to using such a bio-data questionnaire. First of all, it is more easily administered than a test which requires specific testing conditions such as freedom from distraction, exact time limits, and so on. Secondly, the bio-data questionnaire does not require any time in addition to completing the application form because it *is* the application form. Thirdly, recording your data in this form now enables you to do many kinds of studies using background information whenever you want to go into the files. In other words, it renders a wealth of information retrievable. Fourthly, it just makes basic common sense to try to predict future performance systematically by past performance. This is the whole underlying assumption in asking a person about previous work history, academic background, military experience, and so forth. A bio-data form simply allows us to do this in a systematic and empirical way in addition to the informal manner in which we collected information on the application form before the bio-data questionnaire arrived.

A fifth benefit was alluded to before but not pinpointed. The bio-data approach enables management to examine and identify which pieces of information are predicting positive performance in the employees. This means that employers now have a tailor-made series of questions that will predict success in their specific company.

chapter 8

The Future of Personnel Selection Systems

The hire and promotional decisions are here to stay. Court rulings against the specific use of a given test or specific interview questions will not change this fact. The quota system of hiring is fraught with problems, and it is certainly not a long-term solution.

Since the hire and promotional decisions are necessary, the question becomes, "What approaches show the greatest potential for effective selection?" I have said it before, but it is central to my approach and bears repeating: *the solution that is most job-related and best for business will probably be the fairest to minorities.* Stated another way: validated selection systems are good business.

At the risk of overgeneralizing, let me make three observations about the future of personnel selection.

First, the joint use of validated biographical data blanks and scorable interview forms hold wide appeal for *high-census* entry level positions. They are relatively inexpensive. They can be and have been validated (Fleishman and Berniger, 1960). Also, the logic of predicting future performance by using past performance is quite compelling (O'Leary, 1973).

Secondly, the most promising method for selecting supervisory and management personnel from first line supervisors to top management utilizes an approach called Assessment Centers. This method was used during World War II by the Office of Strategic Services and has been refined and systematically validated by American Telephone and Telegraph over the last sixteen years. In that time, AT&T has run over 100,000 people through the program and such major companies as IBM, Sears, J. C. Penney, and Standard Oil of Ohio have installed their own centers.

In the last few years, hundreds of small and medium-sized companies have installed centers. This group includes public employers such as the New York Police Department and the State of Wisconsin (Byham and Wettengel, 1974).

What are Assessment Centers? Basically, the Assessment Center is a series of group and individual exercises which are designed to measure job-related skills and simulate actual on-job activity. They frequently include an interview. *Because they are not as widely used as an interview,* I will discuss the pros and cons of the approach. Basically, they involve one or two days of job simulation exercises with six to twelve participants (candidates) and three to six observers. The observers are picked from line personnel at least one level above the job for which the candidates are being considered, or "target position."

These line managers are thoroughly trained by an Assessment Center Administrator on what to observe during the center schedules. The centers are arranged so that a number of different observers watch the same person during different exercises. This reduces the impact of any subjective bias one observer has for a specific participant on the final results of the center.

After the participants' two days (there are one-day Assessment Centers also) are over, the assessors remain for an additional two days to discuss their observations of each participant and come to some agreement about the observer's ratings on each of a number of key work-related dimensions. These (leadership, analytical skills, judgment, independence, flexibility, and so forth) have been predetermined by the company.

Some centers provide a feedback report to the participant giving him the results of the center's findings. This has been quite helpful and informative to many participants, even to those who perform poorly. Interestingly, studies at IBM show that those who perform poorly at the center do not become disinterested in the organization and feel their career is finished there (Kraut, 1972).

As I see it, Assessment Centers are here to stay because they have a number of substantial benefits:

A. They are job related. The content of many of the exercises closely resembles the kinds of materials found in many managerial and supervisory positions.

B. The approach has been validated in many different companies.

C. Potentially they are acceptable to fair employment agencies. If used properly, the Assessment Center has been proven valid and fair to minorities. In fact, the Assessment Center was agreed upon by both AT&T and the EEOC as a part of the solution in determining which of the thousands of entry level women have supervisory and management potential.

D. Assessment Center results are specific to a given job quality (e.g., judgment, leadership, problem analysis) rather than a gross decision such as go or no-go.

E. Assessment Centers have developmental uses. The results of an Assessment Center pinpoint specific strengths and specific weaknesses, which the candidates need to develop. Consequently, it is a great method for identifying training needs within your organization.

F. Manpower planning can be put to use. Because the results of an Assessment Center give one a clear picture of his people resources, management can do a better job of putting the right person in the job where he can maximally utilize his work skills.

G. Job samples and line managers who are familiar with the job are put to use.

H. It works. (See Bray and Grant, 1966.) When the Assessment Center was initially tried at AT&T (1958), Douglas Bray conducted a mammoth test of the Assessment Center's ability to identify capable from incapable line foreman. This "Management Progress" study has become one of the most significant studies in the field of assessment in the century.

Basically, he evaluated 100 newly hired college graduates and an additional 100 newly hired non-college graduates; and subsequently, he evaluated them using the Assessment Center. The reports generated from these Assessment Centers were locked away for eight years, preventing anyone outside of the center from seeing them.

When the lock was opened and the predictions of the reports compared with actual performance eight years later, the results were impressive. Of the people who were successful as supervisors, the Assessment Center had effectively identified 74 percent eight years prior. Of those who were not successful, the Assessment Center had effectively identified 94 percent.

One reason some companies give for not using the Assessment Center is that the process takes too long—one, two, or three days to observe participants, rather than a half day for interviews. The Assessment Center is primarily used for selecting supervisory and management personnel. It is clearly an involved procedure.

Another point that should be considered in the selection procedure is the use of the job itself as a possible predictor. Many employers in the private and public sectors of our economy have reached for some kind of prediction or test of job success. This was a realistic expectation but has led to an unfortunate reluctance to consider performance on the job as a predictor. The fact is, actual performance on the job is the most effective predictor of future performance.

The reason job performance has not been used as a predictor in the past is an awareness that it would be too expensive to put every candidate on the job and give him a sink-or-swim opportunity. However, your selection system could be used in conjunction with a training program for supervisors. They could be instructed on how to observe the performance of the new employee by counseling during those first days on the job and on how to make systematic observations in writing about the new employee's performance. After a reasonable amount of training time, it should be decided whether the new employee is going to work out or not. (What is reasonable will vary from job to job, but can usually be agreed upon by a group of incumbents and supervisors of other positions in question.)

My point is that many organizations, particularly in the public sector (e.g., cities, states, military, etc.) have a thirty-, sixty-, or ninety-day period where the new employees are on probation. Some organizations have a six month's probation period. In some instances, the new employee does not become a member of the union until this period is over. Apparently many of the organizations are not fully using this test period. A closer look needs to be taken at the method of the ratings given by the supervisor during this period. But if these could become more objective to some degree, if two independent raters of an employee's performance could be used and if specific behavioral examples of their ratings are given, another powerful and job-related tool could be added to your system of selection.

There is little question that the interview will continue to play a major role in the selection decisions of the future. The ease with which it is carried out will insure its wide applicability. The greatest change in this area will be a major thrust to improve the quality, objectivity, and validity of the interview results. These will be more emphasized on scoring the interview and using the appropriate method of asking questions.

One central point that I have tried to stress is the importance of the system approach in making selections. Whether one uses a well-prepared and conducted interview or test, biographical information, or the first impression from looking at a person (and there are probably many selection decisions based on that), there is and must continue to be a growing awareness of the limitations of any one selection procedure. This fact does not, however, negate the importance of improving the interview.

This book has been written in the belief that the ability to interview effectively rests a great deal on using basic common sense and having a few simple tools with which to develop a particular interviewing style. It is my sincere desire that this book will help to bridge the gap between technical knowledge and behavioral science on one hand and day-to-day practical hire decisions on the other.

Patterned
Interview Guide

The following format is a suggested model for a patterned interview guide. The rating section at the end of the form renders the interview a scorable interview. The "weights" column allows one to attach more importance to one or more factors than to others.

Let's assume that supervisory ability is considered important but not as important as the person's motivation to work. This relatively greater importance of motivation to work for this position can be reflected in the final score by a system of score weights. Such a system would assign more weight to a score earned on a more important dimension.

For example, such greater importance could be reflected by multiplying the score earned on motivation to work by 2 while the score earned on supervisory ability would be multiplied by only 1.

Patterned Interview Guide

Name _____ Date _____
     Last   First   Initial
Position applied for _____
_____
_____

AREA I *Motivation for the Job*

| Suggested Questions |
1. What do you want from a job?

_____

_____

2. Where do you want to be five years from now, in terms of your career?

_____

_____

3. Give some examples of projects in which you were highly motivated.

_____

_____

AREA II *Adequacy of Work Experience*

| Suggested Questions |
1. What are the most crucial things you learned on your first few jobs?

_____

_____

2. What experiences on your present (last) job added most to your development?

_____

_____

3. We all have work related strengths, what do you consider to be your three major strengths?

_____

_____

4. Why do you want this job?

_____

_____

5. Why do you think you can do this job?

_____

_____

AREA III *Potential*

| Suggested Questions |

1. Think of the best supervisor you ever had. What made him so good?

_____

_____

2. What characterizes outstanding supervisors?

_____

_____

3. If you were teaching a course in supervision and you could cover only two major points, what would you cover?

_____

_____

4. What sort of supervision most effectively motivates you?

_____

_____

AREA IV *Academic Performance*

| Suggested Questions |
1. What was your academic rank in high school?

_____

2. What particular academic achievement did you have at college?

_____

3. What organizations did you belong to and what positions did you hold in high school and college?

_____

AREA V *Career Decision*
| Suggested Questions |

1. What factors influenced you to choose your present career?

_____

_____

2. What did you hope to be when you were in school?

_____

_____

3. If you had all the money you need, what occupation would you choose?

_____

_____

4. In what ways is your present occupation less than ideal for you?

_____

_____

AREA VI   *Spouse's and Family's Impact on the Job*

1. If I asked your spouse why this job would not be ideal, what would she/he say?

_____

_____

2. What have your spouse's reactions to this possible job and location change been?

_____

_____

3. How do your children view this job?

_____

_____

AREA VII   *Health*

1. What illnesses or accidents have kept you out of school or kept you from working for more

than a couple of days?

_____

_____

2. What precautions has your physician suggested in the past?

_____

_____

4. What accidents have you had?

_____

_____

RATINGS

Performance	Score
Far above average	5
Above average	4
Average	3
Below average	2
Far below average	1

	Weights	Score	Weighted Score
1. How motivated is the person on the job?	_____	_____	_____
2. How job related is the person's work experience?	_____	_____	_____
3. How good is the person's supervisory ability?	_____	_____	_____
4. How effective is the person's ability to work cooperatively with others?	_____	_____	_____

5. How good is the
   candidate's
   vocational
   adjustment?   _____ _____ _____
6. Are there likely
   to be any health
   problems?   _____ _____ _____

Job Analysis

Job Analysis

Identification Number

1. Job Title: _____
2. D.O.T. #: _____
3. Experience: _____

4. Job summary: _____
   _____

5. Description of major tasks: _____
   _____
   _____
   _____

6. Description of tasks performed infrequently:
   _____
   _____

7. Positive critical incidents (In reviewing the performance of others in this job try to recall *specific incidents* that made certain people stand out as above average.):

_____
_____
_____
_____

8. Negative critical incidents (In doing this try to think of *specific incidents* that marked certain people as below average performers.):

_____

_____

_____

_____

9. In your estimation, what are the *essential* qualities for success in this job:

_____

_____

10. What are the desirable qualities (but not essential):

_____

_____

11. Machines, tools, equipment, and work aids: ____

_____

_____

12. Materials and products: _____

_____

_____

13. Training (What is essential? What training is desirable for this job?):

_____

_____

_____

14. Relation to other workers:
      Promotion from _____ to _____
      Transfer from _____ to _____
      Supervision received _____ to _____

_____

15. Definition of terms: _____

_____

16. General comments: _____

_____

_____

_____

_____

_____

17. Analyst _____ Date _____

 Editor _____

 Reviewed by _____

Alternate Sample of Interviewer Worksheet for Skilled Trade Training Program

Alternate Sample of Interviewer Worksheet for Skilled Trade Training Program

Date _____

Candidate's Name: _____

Interviewer's Name: _____

Directions: Using the open-ended question pool Interviewer's Guide as a source of suggested questions, prove the qualities on this worksheet. When you are satisfied the interview has generated sufficient information to rate the candidate on each quality, dismiss him or her before independently rating the applicant.

Job Related Qualities

1. Planning

1	2	3	4	5
Very little quality was shown	Less than average quality shown	Moderate amount of quality shown	Above average of quality shown	Quality in evidence to an outstanding degree

Remarks: _____

_____

_____

2. Ability to get along with people (fellow workers, superiors, customers, etc.)

1	2	3	4	5
Very little quality was shown	Less than average quality shown	Moderate amount of quality shown	Above average of quality shown	Quality in evidence to an outstanding degree

Remarks: _____

_____

3. Attention to details

1	2	3	4	5
Very little quality was shown	Less than average quality shown	Moderate amount of quality shown	Above average of quality shown	Quality in evidence to an outstanding degree

Remarks: _____

_____

4. Ability to understand written and oral communications

1	2	3	4	5
Very little quality was shown	Less than average quality shown	Moderate amount of quality shown	Above average of quality shown	Quality in evidence to an outstanding degree

Remarks: _____

_____

5. Pride in work

1	2	3	4	5
Very little quality was shown	Less than average quality shown	Moderate amount of quality shown	Above average of quality shown	Quality in evidence to an outstanding degree

Remarks: _____

_____

6. Interest in this trade and working with their hands

1	2	3	4	5
Very little quality was shown	Less than average quality shown	Moderate amount of quality shown	Above average of quality shown	Quality in evidence to an outstanding degree

Remarks: _____

_____

7. Overall Rating

0	10	20	30	40	50	60	70	80	90	100

Bibliography

Anderson, C. W. The relation between speaking times and decisions in the employment interview. *Journal of Applied Psychology,* 1960, **44**, 267–268.

AT&T Case, *Fair Employment Practices Cases,* vol. 6, pp. 643–662.

Bellows, R. M., and Estep, M. F. *Employment Psychology: The Interview.* New York: Rinehart, 1954.

Berne, Eric. *Games People Play.* New York: Grove Press, 1964.

Blum, Milton, and Naylor, J. *Industrial Psychology: Its Theoretical and Social Foundations.* 3d ed. New York: Harper and Row, 1968.

Bolster, B. F., and Springbett, B. M. The reaction of interviewers to favorable and unfavorable information. *Journal of Applied Psychology,* 1961, **45**, 97–103.

Bonneau, L. R. An interview for selecting teachers. *Dissertation Abstracts,* 1957, **17**, 537–538.

Bray, D. W., and Grant, D. L. The assessment center in the measurement of potential for business management. *Psychological Monographs,* 1966, 80 (17, Whole No. 625).

Byham, William C., and Wettengel, Carl. Assessment centers for identifying and developing supervisory and management potential in government operations. *Public Personnel Management,* 1974.

Civil Rights Act of 1964 as Amended by Public Law, 92–261. In *Federal Mandates for Affirmative Action,* National Civil Service League, Washington, D.C., 1972.

Daniels, H. W., and Otis, J. L. A method of analyzing employment interviews. *Personnel Psychology,* 1950, **3**, 425–555.

Dictionary of Occupational Titles, 3rd Ed., Washington, D.C., United States Government Printing Office: 1965.

Equal Employment Opportunity Commission. *Guidelines on Employment Testing Procedures.* Washington, D.C.: United States Government Printing Office, 1966.

Fair Employment Practice Cases. Bureau of National Affairs.

Fleishman, Edwin A., and Berniger, J. One way to reduce office turnover. *Personnel,* 1960, **37**, 63–69.

Griggs versus Duke Power Company Case. *Journal Mandates for Affirmative Action.*

Greenspoon, J. The reinforcing effect of two spoken sounds on the frequency of two responses. *American Journal of Psychology,* 1955, **68**, 409–416.

Harris, Thomas. *I'm OK—You're OK.* New York: Harper and Row, 1969.

Keating, E., Patterson, D. G., and Stone, C. H. Validity of work histories obtained by the interview. *Journal of Applied Psychology,* 1950, **34**, 6–11.

Kraut, A. I. A hard look at management assessment centers and their future. *Personnel Journal,* 1972, **51**, 317–326.

Labor Turnover Handbook. Merchants and Manufacturers Association, 1970.

Mayfield, E. C. The selection interview—a re-evaluation of published research. *Personnel Psychology,* 1964, **17**, 239–260.

Mosel, James, and Wade, Richard. A weighted application blank for reduction of turnover in reports with store sales clerks. *Personnel Psychology,* 1951, **4**, 177–184.

New tool: "Reinforcement" for good work. *Business Week,* December 18, 1971.

Odiorne, George S. *Management by Objectives.* New York: Pitman, 1965.

O'Leary, Lawrence R. Is employment testing a thing of the past? *Personnel Journal,* 1972, 51 (3), 170–172.

————. Fair employment, sound psychometric practice, and reality—A dilemma and a partial solution. *American Psychologist,* 1973, 28 (2).

Spriegel, W. R., and James, V. A. Trends in recruitment and selection practices. *Personnel,* 1958, 35 (3), 42–48.

Trankell, A. The psychologist as an instrument of prediction. *Journal of Applied Psychology,* 1959, **43**, 170–175.

Ulrich, L., and Trumbo, D. The selection interview since 1949. *Psychological Bulletin,* 1965, **63**, 100–116.

Verplank, W. S. The control of the content of conversation reinforcement of statements of opinion. *Journal of Abnormal and Social Psychology,* 1955, **51**, 668–676.

Wagner, R. The employment interview: A critical review. *Personnel Psychology,* 1949, **2**, 17–46.

Worell, L. Level of aspiration and academic success. *Journal of Educational Psychology,* 1959, **50**, 47–54.

Weiss, D. J., and Dawis, R. V. An objective validation of factual interview data. *Journal of Applied Psychology,* 1960, **44**, 381–385.

Index